ADVANCE PRAISE

Deborah Kevin's insightful, organized, and information-packed guide is the perfect toolbox for authors at any level. It can easily become an author's number one resource for generating, increasing, and sustaining book sales and loyal readers.

— **LORRAINE DONOHUE BONZELET,
AUTHOR IN THE *MINDFUL WRITERS
RETREAT* ANTHOLOGIES**

An outstanding and essential resource. Deborah Kevin's experience as a publisher has given her deep insight into the ways writers can advocate for themselves and claim agency over their careers' trajectories. For the many writers — like me — for whom marketing sometimes feels like an impossible challenge, *Shelf Life* is game-changing. From more familiar techniques, like building a website, to fresh ideas, like choosing the energy you want to bring to your marketing, Kevin presents proven ways for writers to build their communities and maximize their outreach without sacrificing authenticity. Her supportive, engaging style transforms the potentially-scary into easy-to-understand steps that are not only actionable but exciting. If you're a writer looking to become your own best advocate, this book is for you!

— **KRIS FAATZ, AWARD-WINNING
AUTHOR OF *FOURTEEN STONES***

Deborah Kevin doesn't just talk the talk, but she walks the walk. And I say that both figuratively and literally. She puts her extensive personal writing and publishing experience, as well as her work, to lift other writers up into this remarkable and comprehensive field guide. She speaks the truth to authors, but her straight-shooting methodology still comes with compassion, helping you to gain a step-by-step understanding and offering practical solutions no matter where you are on your writing and publishing journey. Simply, this book is your must-have, no-nonsense, practical over-view of effective and long-term marketing strategies to help propel you to the next level.

— MARK LESLIE LEFEBVRE, AUTHOR
OF *AN AUTHOR'S GUIDE TO WORKING
WITH LIBRARIES AND BOOKSTORES*

Ms. Kevin's *Shelf Life* is both comprehensive and concise, chock full of advice, interesting facts about the publishing industry, and actionable ideas for building a sustainable marketing plan for your books. I especially appreciate the "Ninja Tips" scattered throughout, which highlight best practices on a variety of topics. I will keep *Shelf Life* close by as I level up my author business.

— R.A. JOHNSON, AUTHOR OF THE
ENCLAVE SERIES

If you're searching for insights from a publishing visionary who reveals how to set your book up for success, then *Shelf Life* is the guide for you. Deborah does more than lay the groundwork for why marketing after a book launch is critical. She also provides clear, easy-to-follow steps for those who may feel frozen with indecision on where or how to start. She takes away the guesswork that many authors find themselves trapped in, and her compassionate and encouraging tone emphasizes her genuine desire to see each book find its audience and reach its full potential.

— JENNIA HEROLD D'LIMA

Deborah Kevin's *Shelf Life* provides invaluable "How to" and "Where to" guidance for continuing to spotlight your beloved book after you've completed your launch! Clear, succinct, and doable, it's a must-have for continuing to reach potential readers.

— MARIBETH DECKER, BESTSELLING AUTHOR OF *PEACE IN PASSING: COMFORT FOR LOVING HUMANS DURING ANIMAL TRANSITIONS*

SHELF LIFE

ALSO BY DEBORAH KEVIN

Heart-Centered Marketing: Proven Strategies to Naturally Attract and Nurture Clients

Your First Year: What I Wish I'd Known

You've Written Your Book. Now What?

SHELF LIFE

A Field Guide to Long-Term Author Success

DEBORAH KEVIN

Foreword by
DAN MANZANARES, MFA

HIGHLANDER
PRESS

ISBN: 978-1-956442-50-2
Ebook ISBN: 978-1-956442-53-3
Library of Congress Control Number: Applied For.

Published by Highlander Press
501 W. University Pkwy, Ste. B2
Baltimore, MD 21210

Cover design: Hanne Broter
Author photo: Brenda Jankowski

To my beloved husband and twin flame Rob:
You make everything worthwhile.

CONTENTS

FOREWORD

DAN MANZANARES, MFA

A standard practice for anyone with publishing aspirations should be to receive a copy of Deborah Kevin's *Shelf Life*. Perhaps this person recently graduated from an MFA creative writing program, or landed a contract with a traditional publisher, or decided to go all in as an Indie author. Regardless, in that moment, *Shelf Life* should be bought and handed to them.

As a person transforms themselves from writer to author, meaning their work becomes available for purchase, they're in the making-connections-with-readers business. *However*. Gone are the days when a book had the expectation and the chance to create its own audience. Today's market is simply too big. The hours in a day are too few for any one reader to waste time deciding to become a fan for a newly published book that feels disconnected from its author.

Boiled down: A book's post-launch success is greatly determined by its author's engagement with readers.

This doesn't seem fair. Building a relationship with readers, of course, costs money. The author must allocate wages earned from their day job to finance this relationship. Depending on an author's individual financial situation, the pacing and breadth of their relationship with readers is affected. Still, an author shouldn't feel deterred, and overreact by having zero relationships with readers post-launch. Social media, for example, costs more time than money. Their book, which now exists in the world, is the main connection point to an audience. Readers recognize this existence, but to become an advocate for the book, they require supplemental activity from the book's creator. If a new book is paired with an available author, sales are made. With enough sales, more wages can be allocated to accommodate a growing audience.

Fairness aside, in the situation where an author is nowhere to be found, the sales numbers are known. A few hundred copies (if lucky, a few thousand) sold in the first year, and nothing much afterward. This is true regardless of how an author publishes—whether it's Indie, small press, or large traditional houses. Do those numbers reflect the value of a good book embodied with an author's time and imagination? No. Then, why should any author settle for that type of sales record?

Here, it's important for the author to be clear-headed as to why they're publishing. There are many reasons. Prestige, ego, self-reliance, hope for a big payday, art for art's sake, name legacy, they are famous, they are inherently well-connected in the industry, just to name a few. These are all fine and good. But there's another *why* out there. One explored and delivered by *Shelf Life*.

An author's *why* can be the reader. Their future readers. The people an author brings along with them as co-discovers of the truth about life, death, and the human condition. So, there's a difference between, "I want to sell as many copies as possible," and, "I want to connect with as many readers as I can."

Building relationships with other people is work. It's scary. It's the long game. But your book is worth it!

Shelf Life has given me the toolbox on how best to engage with my readers, as well as the strategy on how to use those tools. For that I'm not only grateful but empowered.

INTRODUCTION

Hurrah! You've written and published your book. The launch went wonderfully, and your friends and family really showed up. However, you may have experienced a visibility hangover post-launch. So you stopped talking about your book (aren't people tired of hearing about it anyway?)...and then, crickets. What should you do next? You have no idea. I hope, after reading this book, that adrift feeling evaporates.

You are not alone. I noticed several things when opening Highlander Press's doors to would-be authors. First, misinformation about the publishing industry and process abounds. Second, the belief that if authors got a traditional publishing deal, they could simply hand off their brilliant manuscript and move on to the next thing without engaging in marketing. Third, there is a lack of understanding that authors love their books more than anyone else—just like a parent's love for their child is greater than anyone else's.

So, I began speaking truth to authors through classes, presentations, interviews, and social media. This book is a culmination of all the wisdom I've gained by writing, editing, and publishing hundreds of books by all kinds of authors. I often say, "This is not the *Field of Dreams*—if you write it, they will not come—unless you tell them your book exists!"

I believe it's crucial to have one's eyes wide open when looking at the realities of writing and publishing a book. My goal in sharing the following statistics is not to discourage you or have you drop your project. On the contrary, I want you to be empowered with facts—so you can make an effective plan to market your book to have the kind of impact you want, whether it's to grow your readership or expand your business or raise awareness. Here are a few "fun" facts:

- Traditionally published nonfiction books average sales of 250-300 copies in the first year.[1]
- Traditionally published debut novels see average sales between 500-3,000 copies sold in the first year.[2] During the antitrust lawsuit regarding Penguin Random House's proposed acquisition of Simon & Schuster, it was revealed that most traditionally published books sell fewer than 250 copies.[3]
- Self-published books sell an average of 250 copies in the first year. However, the majority sell fewer than 100 copies, with only a small percentage achieving higher sales.[4]

But these numbers aren't all doom and gloom. You actually have **more** control than you realize! According to Scribe Media.[5]

- Sales typically decline sharply after the first year *unless ongoing marketing efforts are in place.*
- Consistent engagement with readers and periodic promotional activities are **crucial** to maintaining visibility and sales.

- Authors who invest in long-term marketing strategies, such as building an email list and engaging on social media, tend to see better sales performance over the two-year period.[6,7]

With this book, I'm taking a stand for YOU. I want you to feel so much pride in writing your first—or seventh or twentieth book and getting it out in the world, whether you independently published it, got a traditional pub deal, or worked with a hybrid publisher. The wisdom shared between this book's covers is relevant to every book, every genre, and every author. The tools and insights you gain herein will empower you to take control of your book's longevity and ongoing sales.

Here's the bald truth: You must become an expert marketer. Taking a two-pronged approach is crucial to extending the shelf life of your book:

- **Initial Push:** The first year is critical for setting the foundation for a book's success. Effective launch strategies and initial marketing efforts can significantly impact long-term sales.
- **Ongoing Engagement:** Continued engagement with readers through social media, email newsletters, and promotional events is essential to sustain sales beyond the first year.

You may think, "Who are you, and why should I listen to you?" Fair enough, really! Not only am I an author, but I've graduated from Stanford University's Creative Writing program in Novel Writing (I write historical fiction) and earned a master's degree from Western Colorado University's Graduate Program for Creative Writing with a concentration in publishing. I started my company in 2012 as a marketing copywriting agency before transitioning in 2019 full-time into book editing and publishing. I've also been an editor at *Little Patuxent Review,* a Maryland-based literary journal, and managing editor at Inspired Living Publishing, where I've edited and published eight ILP anthologies. With Highlander Press, I've published dozens of well-received books and am known as a straight-shooter and unfailing supporter of our authors.

I suggest that you read *Shelf Life* from cover to cover. Assess what you're already doing and how well or how consistently you're doing it. Note what feels like low-hanging fruit and implement those tasks next. Think of book marketing as juggling: get a few balls going well and increase your comfort and consistency before adding a new ball to the mix. In some cases, you may first need to return to basics, taking a step backward to catapult yourself forward.

My goal in writing this book is to help you understand your role in marketing your work and learn practical solutions to increasing visibility for your book and you as an author.

I believe in you!

THE BASICS

WHAT DRIVES BUYING DECISIONS?

U nderstanding who your readers are and why they might want your book is worth a brief discussion. Sure, it's possible that someone will just be looking for "a good book" and pick up yours to consider. But your odds of increased sales increase if you mindfully determine where those readers are and how to reach and then nurture them effectively!

Below are the major categories that drive people to make purchases:

- Emotional Connection
- Trust and Brand Reputation
- Price Sensitivity
- Social Proof and Reviews
- Personalization
- Sustainability and Other Ethical Considerations
- Convenience

EMOTIONAL CONNECTION

Do your readers already know-like-trust you? Are they super fans? Are they voracious readers in your genre? A study by the Harvard Business Review found that customers who are emotionally connected to a brand are twice as likely to purchase a product or service, and they tend to be more loyal (e.g., 306% higher lifetime value).

TRUST AND BRAND REPUTATION

If you have a book or a business for which you're writing or have written a book, you have an author brand. That you have an author brand, which we will dig into in a later chapter, is vital to understand. As yourself: Are your fans following you on social media or subscribing to your newsletter? Do you have a reputation for producing superior books? Are you garnering reviews—and sharing them?

According to Edelman's Trust Barometer, 81% of consumers said that they need to trust the brand to do what is right to buy from them. A Nielsen report showed that 92% of consumers trust peer recommendations above all other forms of advertising. This last statistic is one to grasp—your friends, families, and peers will be your best sales force for your book launch and beyond. Don't discount them!

PRICE SENSITIVITY

Post-COVID has seen printing and distribution prices skyrocketing, which may drive more readers to consider digital or library books. A survey by PWC found that price is the primary factor in customer purchase decisions 60% of the time, indicating a significant role in how consumers choose products, including books.

Do you remember in decades past when a hardcover book would be released first and, a year later, the paperback would be published? Devout readers of a particular author or genre snapped up hardbacks as soon as they were published, but others waited a year before making their purchases. Why? Primarily due to price. Hardback books cost more. That's also why digital books have become popular—they cost less to produce and distribute.

> **Ninja Tip:** Determine how your ideal readers like to read and make sure your book is available in that format.

SOCIAL PROOF AND REVIEWS

Amazon, Goodreads, LibraryThing, and other review sites are crucial for your book's longevity. An entire chapter of this book is dedicated to garnering more reviews—and using them effectively! BrightLocal's survey noted that 87% of consumers read online reviews for local businesses in 2020 (yes! you have an author business), up from 81% in 2019, highlighting the growing importance of social proof.

> **Ninja Tip:** Use reviews on social media posts and in your newsletter. And don't be afraid to put them into a rotation!

PERSONALIZATION

Fans want to be seen and acknowledged—sometimes, this can be as easy as sending a handwritten thank you note. According to a report from Epsilon, 80% of consumers are more likely to purchase when brands offer personalized experiences. Think about how you can authentically engage with your readers, offering personal experiences. Can you host live Q&A discussions via Zoom? Send thank you notes? Or offer flat SWAG (stuff we all get), like bookmarks, autographed bookplates, or stickers?

SUSTAINABILITY AND OTHER ETHICAL CONSIDERATIONS

Some readers chose digital books specifically for sustainability reasons. Others want to know a publisher's sustainability and fair-trade practices. If you're that publisher, have you thought about how to communicate these to your readers? A Nielsen study revealed that 73% of global consumers would definitely or probably change their consumption habits to reduce their environmental impact.

CONVENIENCE

How easy is it for readers to discover and purchase your books? A survey by the National Retail Federation found that 97% of respondents have backed out of a purchase because it was inconvenient. If your book is only available in one format, you've increased the inconvenience by limiting how readers can consume it. Publishing your book on only one platform might significantly impair potential sales. Always ask yourself, "How can I make purchasing my books easy?"

The above statistics underscore the multifaceted nature

of buying and investing decisions, where factors like emotional connection, trust, price, personalization, social proof, sustainability, and convenience all play critical roles.

TAPPING INTO EMOTIONS

Emotion in marketing is crucial because it significantly influences reader behavior and decision-making. Here's why integrating emotion into marketing strategies is so effective:

- **Enhanced Memory and Recall**: Emotional content tends to be more memorable than non-emotional content. When readers feel a strong emotion—joy, sadness, fear, or surprise—they are more likely to remember the associated author or book.
- **Building Stronger Brand Connections**: Emotions help to forge deeper connections between an and her readers. When readers emotionally resonate with a marketing message, they often feel a closer affinity to the author, which can foster loyalty and long-term engagement.
- **Influencing Purchasing Decisions**: Many purchasing decisions are not made purely on logic or reasoning but are significantly swayed by how a book or author makes a reader feel. Emotionally charged marketing can persuade readers by appealing to their desires, aspirations, or fears.
- **Differentiation in a Crowded Market**: Emotional marketing can help an author stand out in markets flooded with similar books by creating a unique emotional experience. This can be a critical differentiator that sets one author apart from others.

- **Encouraging Sharing and Virality**: Content that evokes strong emotions is likelier to be shared across social networks. Emotional reactions can drive virality, significantly increasing a campaign's reach and impact beyond the original target audience.
- **Building Brand Advocacy**: Positive emotional experiences can transform satisfied readers into author advocates. People are more likely to recommend an author or book to others if they have an emotional attachment to it.

By tapping into emotions, authors can enhance their marketing strategies and create meaningful, impactful interactions that drive the reader's behavior. Throughout this book, you'll be given specific tools to increase your readers' connection to you and your books.

KNOW YOUR TARGET
READERSHIP

I have a question: "Who are your ideal readers, and where do they hang out?" If you answered, "Anyone would love my book," you're setting yourself up for failure. While technically it's a truth that anyone *could* read your book, specific readers love the genre in which you write. Your job as an author is to know who these readers are and where they hang out. If it helps, consider these readers as characters in your book—create a character brief and give them a name!

Let's illustrate the point. A mini-van-driving professional woman with tweens who loves reading romance will "hang out" in person or online differently than a twenty-something skateboarding, Anime-loving, graphic novel reader. A sixty-something former executive who volunteers annually on a mission trip will "hang out" in different places than a thirty-something vegan who lives off-grid and grows their own food.

Writing a newsletter to a general audience is much harder than writing a letter to your favorite auntie. Why? Because you know your auntie, she's real, has preferences, and will read anything you write. Can you achieve that same kind of intimacy with your fans? You can—simply by knowing them better. This is called reader-centric marketing.

Reader-centric marketing focuses on deeply understanding and catering to your ideal reader, which can significantly enhance engagement, drive sales, and ensure long-term success for your book. By tailoring your content, messaging, and promotional strategies to meet your target audience's specific needs and interests, you create a more personalized and resonant experience that captures their attention and loyalty. This targeted approach increases the likelihood of initial purchases and fosters ongoing relationships with readers who are more likely to become repeat buyers and advocates for your work. Ultimately, a reader-centric strategy helps you build a dedicated community around your book and author brand, sustaining its relevance and success in a competitive market.

IDENTIFYING YOUR IDEAL READER

Defining your audience is a crucial step in effectively marketing your book, and it starts with identifying who your ideal readers are based on genre, themes, and writing style. Begin by analyzing your book's genre— romance, thriller, fantasy, or nonfiction—since each genre tends to attract a specific demographic with distinct preferences.

Next, consider the themes you explore in your writing; for example, a novel focused on personal growth and self-discovery might resonate with readers seeking inspiration and emotional depth. Finally, evaluate your writing style— poetic and descriptive or fast-paced and action-oriented—as it can significantly influence the type of reader drawn to your work. By combining these elements, you can create a clear profile of your ideal reader, allowing you to craft targeted marketing strategies that speak directly to their interests and needs, ultimately enhancing engagement and boosting sales.

DEMOGRAPHICS AND PSYCHOGRAPHICS

Demographics and psychographics are two key concepts in understanding and segmenting your audience, but they focus on different aspects of a population. While demographics tell you who your audience is, psychographics explain why they behave the way they do.

Demographics are more concrete and easier to quantify, providing a broad overview of your audience. Psychographics are more nuanced and qualitative, offering deeper insights into the emotional and psychological factors influencing decision-making. Combining both gives you a comprehensive understanding of your audience, enabling you to create more targeted and effective marketing strategies.

Demographics refer to a population's statistical characteristics that influence reader preferences. These include measurable data such as age, gender, income, education level, marital status, occupation, and location. Demographic information helps you categorize your audience based on common physical or socio-economic traits. For example, a demographic profile might describe a target audience as "women aged twenty-five to thirty-five with a college education living in urban areas."

Psychographics, on the other hand, delve into your audience's psychological attributes. This includes interests, attitudes, values, lifestyles, and behavior. Psychographics help you understand why people make certain choices, what motivates them, and what they care about. For example, a psychographic profile might describe an audience as "health-conscious individuals who value sustainability and are motivated by environmental concerns."

RESEARCHING YOUR READER

Researching your reader is essential to creating effective marketing strategies that resonate with your target audience. To accomplish this, start by gathering demographic and psychographic data to build a profile of your ideal reader.

Utilize surveys, social media insights, and reader interviews to collect valuable information about your audience's preferences, motivations, and behaviors. This research helps you understand who your readers are and what they value, allowing you to tailor your content, messaging, and promotional efforts to meet their specific needs.

ANALYZING READER BEHAVIOR

Once you have a clear profile of your readers, the next step is to analyze their behavior to refine your marketing strategy further. Several tools and platforms can help you track and understand reader behavior:

Website Analytics: Tools like Google Analytics provide detailed insights into how readers interact with your website. You can track metrics such as page views, time spent on pages, bounce rates, and conversion rates to understand which content resonates most with your audience. Additionally, you can see your website traffic sources, helping you identify where your readers are coming from and which marketing channels are most effective.

Social Media Metrics: Social media platforms like Facebook Insights, Instagram Analytics, and Twitter Analytics provide valuable data on how your readers interact with your content. You can track metrics such as likes, shares, comments, follower growth, and post reach to understand what types of content engage your audience. Social media analytics also help you identify the best times to post and which platforms your audience prefers, enabling you to refine your social media strategy for maximum impact. Another incredible tool that pulls all your social media insights into one platform, showing you by platform when your best time to post is, is Metricool.

Email Engagement: Email marketing platforms like Mailchimp, MailerLite, or ActiveCampaign offer analytics that show how your subscribers engage with your emails. Metrics such as open rates, click-through rates, and unsubscribe rates provide valuable feedback on the effectiveness of your email content. By segmenting your email list based on engagement, you can tailor your messaging to different reader groups, improving overall engagement and conversion rates.

Purchasing Patterns: Analyzing purchasing patterns through e-commerce platforms or sales data can reveal which products or books are most popular among your readers. This information helps you understand what drives your readers to make a purchase, allowing you to optimize your pricing, promotional offers, and product positioning. Additionally, tracking repeat purchases can help identify your most loyal customers and provide opportunities for upselling or cross-selling related products.

By leveraging these tools and platforms, you can better understand your readers' behaviors and preferences, enabling you to refine your marketing efforts for better results and long-term success.

YOUR IDEAL READER AVATAR

Knowing who your ideal readers are is crucial for effectively marketing your book because it allows you to tailor your promotional strategies to the specific needs, interests, and behaviors of the people most likely to buy and enjoy your work. Understanding your target audience helps you craft compelling messages that resonate with them, choose the right platforms to reach them, and create content that speaks directly to their desires and challenges. By focusing your efforts on the right audience, you increase the chances of building a loyal readership, driving word-of-mouth promotion, and achieving long-term sales success.

The best way I know how to identify your readers is by visualizing who they are and "interviewing" with them. If you have an established pool of devoted readers already, you might use some of these prompts in social media posts to learn even more about them! Here are just a few reasons why it's crucial to spend time learning about your ideal reader:

- Knowing WHO your ideal reader is helps you determine WHERE they hang out in real life and on social media.
- You can leverage this information to focus your marketing efforts rather than doing the "whack-a-mole" approach to marketing.
- This knowledge helps when writing newsletters, emails, and posts—you're speaking to ONE person instead of the faceless many.

Know that you may have multiple ideal readers—that's okay. You can create more than one avatar, but understand that this makes your job of writing and posting much more difficult. Also, just because you select one avatar to market your book to does not mean that other people different from your avatar won't love and buy your books. It's counterintuitive, I know. But, it's a truth.

Consider these areas when creating your ideal reader avatar:

- Demographics
- Psychographics
- Physical appearance
- Work and Hobbies

DEMOGRAPHICS

- Age
- Gender
- Hair color/eye color
- Location (city, state, country)
- Education
- Income
- Career
- Married or single?
- What kind of car do they drive?

PSYCHOGRAPHICS

- Mac or PC? iPhone, Android, or Windows? iPad or Android tablet?
- Do they like to travel? If yes, where do they like to go?

- Is their favorite Saturday night spent partying on the town or at home with friends?
- Favorite places to shop
- What is their favorite type of restaurant?
- Beer or wine? Coffee or tea?
- What causes or things are they passionate about?
- What is their favorite guilty pleasure?
- What the luxuries they can't live without?

PHYSICAL APPEARANCE

- Male or female or nonbinary?
- How do they dress?
- What's their favorite item of clothing?

Ninja Tip: Give your avatar a name.

WORK AND HOBBIES

- What are their interests?
- Do they have any hobbies?
- What magazines do they read?
- Favorite books/movies/TV/music
- Their favorite social media platforms
- What do they do in their spare time?

This exercise may seem pedantic, but I promise you that knowing your ideal reader will dramatically improve your marketing, which in turn will support better sales.

CONNECTING WITH YOUR READER

Connecting with your reader is essential for building a loyal and engaged audience that will support your work over time. This connection goes beyond simply sharing content; it involves understanding your readers' needs, preferences, and values to create a relationship based on trust and mutual respect.

Connecting with your readers fosters a sense of community and belonging, making them feel valued and heard. This relationship encourages readers to engage with your current work and become advocates for your brand, sharing your content with others and eagerly anticipating your future projects. A strong connection with your readers is the foundation for long-term success, driving immediate engagement and sustained interest in your work.

Tailoring Content to Reader Preferences.
Tailoring your content to align with your readers' preferences is essential for creating a solid connection with your audience. Understand their needs, interests, and expectations to resonate with your ideal readers. For example, if your readers prefer detailed, immersive storytelling, adjust your tone and narrative style to be more descriptive and emotionally engaging. Conversely, if they favor quick, actionable insights, consider adopting a more concise and direct writing style.

Customize your messaging by incorporating themes and topics that resonate with their values and experiences. For instance, if your audience is environmentally conscious, weaving sustainability themes into your content can enhance its relevance and appeal.

You increase engagement and build a loyal readership that feels understood and valued by consistently aligning your content, tone, and messaging with your readers' preferences.

Building Reader Relationships. Building meaningful relationships with your readers is a cornerstone of long-term success as an author. Engaging with your audience through social media, newsletters, and events creates ongoing interaction and connection opportunities. On social media, respond to comments, ask questions, and share behind-the-scenes content that invites readers into your creative process. Personalized newsletters can deepen this connection by offering exclusive content, early access to new releases, and personalized recommendations based on reader interests.

Hosting events, whether virtual or in-person, such as book signings, live Q&A sessions, or writing workshops, provides a platform for direct interaction and fosters a sense of community among your readers. These strategies enhance reader engagement and create a loyal fanbase that actively supports and promotes your work.

Reader Feedback Loops. Incorporating reader feedback into your marketing and content strategies is crucial for continuous improvement and sustained success. Reader feedback loops involve regularly gathering insights from your audience and using this information to refine your approach. This can be achieved through surveys, social media polls, or direct communication, where you ask readers about their preferences, what they enjoy, and what they think could be improved. Analyzing this feedback allows you to identify trends and areas where your content or messaging may need adjustment.

By responding to reader feedback—whether it's adjusting the pacing of your story, addressing common concerns, or introducing new elements that readers have expressed interest in—you demonstrate that you value their input, which can significantly increase reader satisfaction and loyalty. Moreover, maintaining an open dialogue with your audience ensures that your content remains relevant and engaging, ultimately contributing to your long-term success as an author.

ADAPTING TO CHANGING READER DYNAMICS

Adapting to changing reader dynamics is crucial for maintaining relevance and ensuring long-term success as an author. Reader preferences and behaviors can shift due to various factors, including cultural trends, technological advancements, and evolving social values. Staying attuned to these changes allows you to adjust your content, marketing strategies, and engagement methods to meet your audience's current needs.

For example, the rise of digital reading platforms and audiobooks has changed how readers consume content, prompting authors to diversify their formats. Additionally, shifts in social values may influence the themes and topics that resonate with readers, requiring you to align your messaging with these evolving interests.

By continuously monitoring and responding to these dynamics, you can keep your work relevant, deepen your connection with readers, and stay competitive in a rapidly changing literary landscape, thus future-proofing your marketing strategy.

THE POWER OF KNOWING YOUR READER

Understanding and knowing your reader is a powerful tool that can significantly enhance your success as an author. By deeply understanding your audience's needs, preferences, and behaviors, you can tailor your content, messaging, and marketing strategies to resonate with them personally.

This connection fosters reader loyalty, drives engagement, and creates a community that supports and promotes your work. Moreover, knowing your reader allows you to adapt to changing dynamics, ensuring your content remains relevant and impactful over time. Ultimately, the power of knowing your reader lies in its ability to transform your relationship with your audience from transactional to transformational, leading to sustained success and a lasting legacy.

WHAT DOES ENERGY HAVE
TO DO WITH IT?

In today's dynamic marketing landscape, the energy you bring to your strategies can significantly impact your success. This chapter delves into the nuanced differences between leveraging masculine and feminine energies in your marketing approach. While masculine energy is often associated with action, competition, and assertiveness, feminine energy embraces creativity, collaboration, and intuition.

Understanding how to balance these energies can help you create more effective, holistic marketing strategies that resonate deeply with your audience. This chapter explores how aligning your marketing efforts with these energies can lead to more authentic connections, greater engagement, and long-term success.

MASCULINE VERSUS FEMININE ENERGY IN MARKETING

We've all seen images of the stereotypical used car salesman, right? Sometimes, they're considered sleazy, dishonest, pushy, and not someone we'd choose to do business with. Personally,

I visualize a guy I once saw in New York City's Washington Square Park. Picture this: it was late at night, and he wore a traditional tan trench coat, unbelted as he approached potential customers, flashing them to display the various wares dangling inside the coat. "Check it out. Check it out. Rolex. Joints," he chanted as he walked up to passersby. It's an image I haven't been able to shake off, even thirty years later! The whole point of these examples is they aren't effective marketing techniques!

I want to introduce, possibly reintroduce, the notion that marketing serves your readers. To do so effectively, we must first explore the differences between masculine and feminine energy and their relationship to marketing. To be clear, one type of energy is NOT better than the other. We all use both types of energy, so it's a matter of focus, intention, and balance.

Masculine Energy:

- Assertive, logical, competitive, and structured.
- Action-oriented and goal-focused, emphasizing doing over being.
- Values independence, leadership, and decisiveness.

Feminine Energy:

- Nurturing, intuition, empathy, and collaboration.
- Focuses more on being and experiencing rather than doing.
- Values connection, emotion, and receptivity.

TRADITIONAL MARKETING: MASCULINE ENERGY

Traditional advertising and promotion methods aim to reach a broad audience through print, broadcast, direct mail, and outdoor advertising. This approach typically focuses on pushing products or services to consumers using persuasive messaging, emphasizing achieving high visibility and sales volume—think Mad Men! It is often characterized by its one-way communication style, where interaction between the brand and the consumer is minimal, prioritizing reach and frequency over personalized engagement. In short, traditional marketing practices leverage masculine energy.

Masculine marketing techniques, typically focused on products, include:

- Chasing and landing
- Cold calling
- Direct mail
- Aggressive funnels

The pros of leveraging masculine energy are:

- Direct and action-oriented
- Clear and measurable
- Establishes authority

The associated cons include:

- Can feel pushy
- Quicker return on investment (ROI)
- Lower engagement
- Lacks personal connection

NONTRADITIONAL MARKETING: FEMININE ENERGY

Nontraditional marketing emphasizes building genuine, empathetic connections with consumers. It prioritizes understanding and addressing the emotional and relational needs of the audience, often focusing on values such as authenticity, transparency, and community. This strategy seeks to create lasting customer relationships by aligning brand messages and actions with a deep sense of purpose and integrity. It moves beyond mere transactions to foster loyalty and meaningful engagement and leverages feminine energy.

Feminine marketing practices, typically focused on relationships, include:

- Warm introductions
- Nurture campaigns
- Service-minded
- People-centric

The pros of leveraging feminine energy are:

- Stronger customer relationships
- Enhanced brand image
- Increased customer engagement
- Long-term success
- Alignment with modern consumer expectations

The associated cons include:

- More time and resource investment
- Slower return on investment (ROI)
- Misinterpretation risk
- Limited scale

- Potential brand vulnerability

In this book, we'll lead with feminine energy and appropriately lean into masculine energy to extend the life of your book. Why? Leading with feminine energy in marketing means focusing on relationship-building, nurturing connections, and empathy-driven strategies. Feminine energy is collaborative, intuitive, and patient, but masculine energy—directness, assertiveness, and action—can complement these approaches when appropriate.

Ninja Tip: Unsure of your dominant energy? Pay attention to your language as it will offer clues.

Here are practical ways to effectively lead with feminine energy while incorporating masculine energy:

STORYTELLING FIRST, THEN CALL TO ACTION

Feminine Energy: Begin by sharing your story, the inspiration behind your book, or the journey you've been on. This builds emotional connection and trust with your audience.

Masculine Energy: After engaging readers with your story, offer a clear, actionable next step, like signing up for your newsletter or purchasing your book.

ENGAGE IN CONVERSATIONS, THEN AN OFFER

Feminine Energy: Start by asking your audience

open-ended questions on social media or through email, inviting discussion and feedback.

Masculine Energy: Once you've listened and built rapport, follow up with an assertive solution—such as recommending your book or service as a resource that directly addresses their needs.

BUILD COMMUNITY, THEN OPPORTUNITIES

Feminine Energy: Focus on fostering a supportive community by hosting book clubs, virtual events, or collaborative workshops encouraging dialogue and participation.

Masculine Energy: Once the community is engaged, offer a clear path to action, such as inviting attendees to purchase signed copies of your book or to join a paid course.

NURTURE THROUGH EMAIL, THEN PROMOTIONS

Feminine Energy: Send regular, nurturing emails with valuable content—personal stories, behind-the-scenes looks, or helpful tips. This keeps the connection alive.

Masculine Energy: Periodically, include bold, action-oriented promotions, like time-sensitive discounts or special offers that encourage immediate engagement.

COLLABORATE, THEN CONVERT

> **Feminine Energy**: Partner with other authors, bloggers, or influencers to co-create content, such as interviews, guest posts, or collaborative giveaways. This encourages relationship-building and mutual support.

> **Masculine Energy**: After the collaboration, guide your audience to a direct action—buying your book, following you on social media, or attending an event.

By leading with feminine energy, you focus on creating authentic connections. When the time is right, you can strategically bring in masculine energy to drive action. This balance ensures that your marketing feels both genuine and effective.

YOUR AUTHOR
PLATFORM

BUILD YOUR AUTHOR PLATFORM

A robust author platform is essential for long-term success in the literary world. Most, if not all, of these parts of your author platform, ought to have been built before your book launch. If they weren't, there's no time like the present! Unlike promoting a single book, an author platform focuses on establishing your presence and reputation as a writer, allowing you to connect with readers, industry professionals, and influencers on a deeper level. This chapter explores the key components of an effective platform, including your website, social media presence, email list, and professional network.

By building and maintaining a platform centered on you as an author rather than on a specific book, you create a versatile foundation that supports not just your current work but also future projects, helping to sustain your career and engage your audience over the long term.

WHAT MAKES UP YOUR AUTHOR PLATFORM?

An author platform establishes your presence and credibility as a writer. Here are the key components:

- Professional Website
- Social Media
- An Email List
- Network with Other Writers and Industry Professionals
- Create Valuable Content
- Engage with Your Audience
- Utilize SEO and Analytics

By focusing on these key areas, you can build a strong, sustainable author platform that supports your current projects, helps you grow your readership, and advances your career over time. Remember, building an author platform is an ongoing process that requires time, effort, and consistency.

YOUR AUTHOR WEBSITE

Your website serves as the central hub for all your online activities. It should include a professional bio, a blog, a portfolio of your work, and a way for readers to contact you or sign up for your newsletter. Ensure your website is user-friendly, visually appealing, and regularly updated with fresh content. Linking one of your social media accounts, like Instagram, to your website can ensure that you're driving up "hits" on your site, thus increasing its "Google juice." Writing and publishing a blog is another excellent way to highlight your website regularly.

ELEMENTS OF A SIMPLE AUTHOR WEBSITE

A well-structured website includes several key elements:

Book Section

- **Purpose:** The book section is where you showcase your published works. This should include book descriptions, cover images, purchase links, and related content like reviews or excerpts. If you have more than one book, always prioritize the newest one, ensuring the book faces toward the text and not away (having one's book face away from the text indicates subconsciously that you're rejecting your work).

- **Best Practices:** Include links to where your books can be purchased, such as Amazon, Barnes & Noble, or independent bookstores. Add a section for reviews and endorsements to lend credibility.

ABOUT THE AUTHOR

- **Purpose:** This section introduces readers to you, the author. It should provide a brief biography, your writing journey, and personal insights that help readers connect with you. Be sure to show your personality—readers want to know you, not read a list of credentials (if you want them to know your credentials, send them to LinkedIn).
- **Best Practices**: Include a professional author photo, career highlights, and awards or recognition. Personal anecdotes that relate to your writing can also make this section more engaging.

CONTACT

- **Purpose:** The contact section allows readers, media, and potential collaborators to contact you directly.
- **Best Practices:** Provide a simple contact form,

links to your social media profiles, and possibly a dedicated email address for inquiries.

OPTIONAL: MEDIA SECTION

- **Purpose:** A media section is ideal for providing press kits, often called electronic press kits (EPK), and making it easier for journalists, bloggers, and other media professionals to cover your work. You can download a free guide to creating an EPK here: https://highlanderpressbooks.com/only-guide-you-need/.
- **Content:** Include a downloadable press kit with your biography, high-resolution author photos, book covers, press releases, blurbs, reviews, and any past media coverage or interviews. You might also offer sample chapters or other excerpts for media use. Additionally, include links to any video interviews, podcasts, or recorded readings.

OPTIONAL: RESOURCES SECTION

- **Purpose:** A resources section can provide valuable materials for educators, parents, and book clubs, making your site a go-to place for those looking to engage with your work on a deeper level.
- **Content:** Depending on your audience, this section could include reading guides, discussion questions for book clubs, lesson plans for teachers, activities for children, or educational resources that tie into your book's themes. For example, if you write historical fiction, you might offer

timelines or historical background material. You could include printable activities or crafts if your book targets young readers.

Ninja Tip: If you add a plug-in for a social media app like Instagram to your website, every post you make to that social media platform shows up as a "hit" to your website, which gives it great Google juice!

PROS AND CONS: ONE PAGE VS. MULTIPLE PAGES

When building your author website, deciding whether to use a single-page or multi-page layout is essential:

One-Page. A one-page website is commonly referred to as a single-page website or single-page application (SPA). This type of site consolidates all essential information into one continuous scrolling page rather than dividing content across multiple pages. It's often used for portfolios, product show-cases, or landing pages to create a seamless, focused user experience. Your web designer can add a menu linked to various areas on your one-page so that users can quickly "jump" to the section they want.

Pros:

- **Simplicity:** Easier to navigate, especially for readers looking for quick information.
- **Mobile-Friendly:** Single-page designs often work better on mobile devices, offering a smooth scrolling experience.

- **Speed:** One-page websites can load faster, reducing the risk of losing visitors due to slow loading times.

Cons:

- **Limited Content:** Fitting all necessary information without overcrowding the page can be challenging.
- **SEO Challenges:** One-page sites can struggle with SEO because there are fewer opportunities to target multiple keywords.

Multiple Pages. A multiple-page website is designed to organize content across different pages, each dedicated to a specific topic or section, such as About, Services, Contact, and Blog. This structure allows for a more detailed and expansive presentation of information, making it ideal for authors, businesses, and organizations with a wide range of offerings. Multiple-page sites are user-friendly, providing easy navigation and an efficient way for visitors to access relevant content. This type of website is essential for projects requiring depth, scalability, and a more complex user experience.

Pros:

- **Organization:** Allows you to categorize content effectively, making it easier for visitors to find specific information.
- **SEO Advantage:** Multiple pages enable you to optimize each page for different keywords, improving overall visibility.

- **Scalability:** As you publish more books or add more content, a multi-page site can grow with you, providing dedicated spaces for new information.

Cons:

- **Navigation Complexity:** Clear navigation is required to ensure users can easily find what they're looking for.
- **Maintenance:** More pages mean more content to manage, update, and maintain over time.

BEST PLATFORMS FOR AN AUTHOR WEBSITE

When it comes to building a professional and effective author website, choosing the right platform is crucial. While there are many options available, I strongly recommend investing in a WordPress.org website, paired with a Divi template, and hiring a professional to bring your vision to life.

WordPress.org offers unparalleled flexibility, control, and scalability, making it the best choice for authors who want to grow their online presence. The Divi template, known for its versatility and ease of customization, allows for a visually stunning and highly functional site that can adapt to your evolving needs.

By working with a professional, you ensure that your website is beautifully designed and optimized for performance, security, and user experience—ultimately providing a solid foundation for your author platform.

Ninja Tip: Google your favorite authors who write in the same genre and check out their websites. What do you like? Are they easy to use? Is there a call to action?

WORDPRESS

When choosing between WordPress.org and WordPress.com, it's essential to consider your long-term goals, technical expertise, and the level of control you want over your website.

WordPress.org is often referred to as the "self-hosted" version. With WordPress.org, you download the WordPress software and host it on your own server or through a hosting provider. This option offers full control over your website, including the ability to install custom themes and plugins, access to your site's code, and the freedom to monetize your site in any way you choose. It's ideal for authors who plan to grow their site over time and need flexibility, especially if you want to build a complex site with advanced features. However, it also requires you to handle your own security, backups, and maintenance, which can be challenging for beginners.

WordPress.com, on the other hand, is a hosted service that takes care of the technical aspects for you, including hosting, security, and backups. It's easier to set up and use, especially for those who are less tech-savvy, and is often chosen by authors who prefer simplicity and don't need extensive customization options. WordPress.com offers a range of pricing plans, from free to premium, with varying levels of customization and features. However, it comes with limitations: fewer theme and plugin options, restrictions on monetization, and less control over your site's backend.

- **Pros:** Highly customizable with a vast selection of plugins, strong SEO capabilities, and scalable for growth.
- **Cons:** Can be complex for beginners; some advanced features require coding knowledge.

SQUARESPACE

Squarespace is a user-friendly website-building platform known for its beautifully designed templates and all-in-one functionality. Squarespace allows you to create a professional website without coding or technical expertise. With its easy drag-and-drop interface, built-in e-commerce tools, and powerful integrations, you can seamlessly build and customize your website to showcase your work, sell products, and connect with your audience.

- **Pros:** Easy to use with beautiful, professional templates, all-in-one platform with hosting and domain options.
- **Cons:** Limited customization compared to WordPress, slightly more expensive.

WIX

Wix is a versatile website-building platform that offers a simple, drag-and-drop interface, making it accessible for users of all skill levels. With a wide variety of customizable templates, Wix allows you to create a professional and visually appealing website without any coding experience. Wix also offers built-in tools for SEO, e-commerce, and marketing, giving you everything you need to manage your site and grow your audience with ease.

- **Pros:** Very user-friendly with drag-and-drop design, good selection of templates, no coding required.
- **Cons:** Less robust SEO features, can be less flexible for advanced users.

By carefully selecting the right elements and structure for your author platform, you can create an effective online presence that not only promotes your books but also connects you with readers and the literary community. Whether you choose a one-page or multi-page site depends on your content needs and growth plans, but ensuring that it is well-organized, easy to navigate, and visually appealing is key to making a lasting impression.

SOCIAL MEDIA STRATEGIES FOR AUTHORS

In today's digital age, social media has become indispensable for authors looking to connect with their audience, build their brand, and promote their work. This chapter will explore how to effectively harness the power of platforms like Instagram, Threads, YouTube, TikTok, Facebook, and LinkedIn to engage with readers, grow your following, and drive book sales.

By leveraging social media, authors can create a dynamic and interactive presence that goes beyond traditional marketing, allowing for real-time communication and the ability to cultivate a loyal community of fans. This chapter delves into the best practices for each platform, offering practical tips on content creation, audience engagement, and the importance of authenticity in building a successful author brand online.

Here are the latest user statistics as of early 2024, population sizes, and growth rates for the major social media platforms.[8, 9, 10]

Instagram

- Monthly Active Users: Two billion.
- Growth: Instagram continues to grow steadily, though its growth rate has slowed compared to previous years.
- Audience: Primarily younger users aged eighteen to thirty-five, strongly focused on visual content.

Threads

- Monthly Active Users: 175 million.
- Growth: Threads saw rapid growth, reaching 100 million sign-ups within the first five days of its launch, capitalizing on discontent with Twitter post-Musk acquisition.
- Audience: Similar to Instagram, but more text-focused, appealing to users who prefer microblogging.

Facebook

- Monthly Active Users: 3.07 billion.
- Growth: Facebook remains the largest social media platform by user base, though its growth has stabilized, with most new users coming from outside North America and Europe.
- Audience: Broad user base with a slight skew towards users aged thirty-five and older.

TikTok

- Monthly Active Users: 1.04 billion globally, with a potential ad reach of 1.6 billion adults.

- Growth: TikTok is one of the fastest-growing platforms, especially popular among Gen Z and younger Millennials.
- Audience: Primarily younger users, with strong engagement due to its short-form, creative video content.

YouTube

- Monthly Active Users: 2.5 billion.
- Growth: YouTube remains a dominant platform for long-form video content, with consistent growth across all demographics.
- Audience: Diverse, with significant usage across all age groups, making it a versatile platform for creators.

LinkedIn

- Registered Members: 1.1 billion (not all are active monthly users).
- Growth: LinkedIn continues to grow, particularly in professional and business-focused sectors.
- Audience: Professionals, predominantly aged 30 and above, with a focus on networking, industry news, and professional development.

THESE PLATFORMS EACH HAVE UNIQUE AUDIENCES AND strengths, making them powerful tools for authors and marketers to connect with their target readers. Understanding the demographics and growth trends of each platform can help in selecting the right channels for your marketing strategies.

A WORD ABOUT HASHTAGS

A hashtag is a word or phrase preceded by the "#" symbol (e.g., #WritingCommunity) used on social media platforms to categorize content, making it easier for users to find posts related to specific topics or themes. Hashtags help increase the visibility of your posts by connecting them with broader conversations or trends. When users click on or search for a hashtag, they can see all public posts tagged with that keyword, enabling them to discover content beyond their immediate network. Hashtags are widely used on platforms like Instagram, Twitter, TikTok, and LinkedIn to organize content and enhance user engagement.

Using the right hashtags can significantly enhance the visibility of your content, but it's essential to research them before use. Some hashtags become oversaturated or "dead," meaning they no longer effectively reach a broad audience. Tools like Hashtagify, Display Purposes, or the native analytics tools on platforms can help you find the most effective and relevant hashtags. Regularly updating your hashtag strategy ensures your content remains discoverable and engages the right audience.

INSTAGRAM

A visual-centric social media platform where users share photos and videos, often enhanced with filters and captions. It's widely used for personal expression, brand building, and influencer marketing.

Audience Demographics: Instagram's user base skews younger, with many of its users aged eighteen to thirty-four. It is a highly visual platform, making it ideal for authors leveraging strong imagery to complement their written content.

Pros:

- Visual Storytelling: Great for authors who can use images and videos to enhance their stories.
- High Engagement: Instagram boasts high engagement rates, particularly with younger audiences.
- Hashtags: Hashtags are crucial on Instagram for reaching a broader audience. Popular hashtags for authors include #AmWriting, #Bookstagram, #AuthorLife, and #IndieAuthor.

Cons:

- Time-Consuming: Requires consistent content creation and engagement.
- Limited Link Sharing: Only one link is allowed in the bio, making driving traffic directly from posts difficult.
- Best For: Authors with a strong visual element to their work or those who can create compelling images and videos. Also great for engaging with younger readers and the Bookstagram community.

Hashtags: Research is crucial as some hashtags become oversaturated or "dead," meaning they don't reach a broad audience due to overuse or being banned. Tools like Display Purposes or Hashtagify can help identify effective hashtags.

THREADS

A text-based social media platform launched by Meta, designed for brief, conversational posts similar to Twitter, with a focus on fostering discussions and community engagement. Once Elon Musk purchased Twitter, there was a mass exodus from that platform to Threads.

Audience Demographics: Threads, a text-based app launched by Meta, is still emerging and appeals to users who enjoy Twitter-style microblogging. The demographic is similar to Instagram but with a focus on text and discussion rather than images.

Pros:

- Text-Focused: Ideal for authors who excel at engaging discussions and short-form writing.
- Cross-Platform Integration: Seamlessly integrates with Instagram, allowing for easy cross-posting.

Cons:

- New Platform: As a newer platform, it's still building its user base and engagement metrics.
- Limited Features: Currently needs some of the advanced features of other platforms, like hashtags and rich media integration.
- Best For: Authors who want to engage in quick, conversational posts and connect with readers in a more casual, text-focused environment.

Hashtags: Threads does not support hashtags at this time, so focus on direct engagement and discussions.

FACEBOOK

One of the largest social media platforms globally, Facebook allows users to connect with friends and family, join groups, share posts, and engage with various content, including news, videos, and events.

Audience Demographics: Facebook has a broad user base, but it is particularly popular among users aged thirty-five and older, making it ideal for reaching an older demographic.

Pros:

- Wide Reach: Facebook's extensive user base provides access to a diverse audience.
- Community Building: Features like groups and events allow for the creation of engaged communities around specific topics or books.

Cons:

- Algorithm Changes: Facebook's algorithm can make it difficult for posts to reach followers without paid promotion.
- Content Saturation: The platform is saturated with content, making it harder to stand out.
- Best For: Authors targeting an older demographic or those interested in creating and managing active reader communities.

Hashtags: While hashtags can be used on Facebook, they are not as effective as on Instagram or Twitter. Instead, focus on creating engaging posts and leveraging Facebook groups.

TIKTOK

A RAPIDLY GROWING VIDEO-SHARING PLATFORM KNOWN for its short, engaging videos set to music or sound bites, popular among younger audiences for creative content and viral trends. For authors, creating short videos highlighting their lives, their work, where they write, and who they are work great!

Audience Demographics: TikTok is wildly popular among Gen Z and younger Millennials, with a large user base aged sixteen to twenty-four. It's a video-centric platform with a focus on short, engaging content.

Pros:

- High Viral Potential: TikTok's algorithm favors content that keeps viewers engaged, offering high potential for virality.
- Creative Content: Allows for creativity in presenting books through short videos, challenges, and trends.

Cons:

- Content Creation Demands: Requires frequent video content, which can be time-consuming.

- Youth-Centric: May not be as effective for reaching older audiences.
- Best For: Authors with a knack for video content or those targeting younger audiences. Particularly effective for genres like YA, fantasy, and romance.

Hashtags: Essential for discovery on TikTok. Popular ones include #BookTok, #BookRecommendations, and #BookLover. Like Instagram, researching active hashtags is important to avoid dead or oversaturated ones.

YOUTUBE

The largest video-sharing platform where users can upload, watch, and interact with video content ranging from tutorials and vlogs to music videos and live streams, making it ideal for both creators and consumers of long-form content.

Audience Demographics: YouTube has a diverse user base, with strong appeal across all age groups, particularly eighteen to forty-nine. It's ideal for long-form video content, including tutorials, interviews, and book trailers.

Pros:

- Long-Form Content: Great for deep dives into topics, book discussions, or author vlogs.
- SEO Friendly: YouTube videos rank well in search engines, offering long-term visibility.
- Monetization Opportunities: Authors can monetize their content through ads, sponsorships, and memberships.

Cons:

- High-Production Effort: Creating quality video content requires more time and resources than other platforms.
- Consistency Needed: Regular uploads are crucial to maintaining and growing an audience.
- Best For: Authors who can create engaging long-form content or wish to build a personal brand through vlogs, tutorials, or in-depth discussions.

Hashtags: Hashtags on YouTube are less central but can still be useful. Focus on SEO-friendly titles and descriptions, using relevant hashtags like #AuthorTube, #BookReview, or #WritingTips.

LINKEDIN

A professional networking platform that focuses on career development, industry discussions, and business-related content, making it ideal for professionals, businesses, and nonfiction authors.

Audience Demographics: LinkedIn is geared towards professionals, with a user base mostly aged thirty and above. It's ideal for nonfiction authors or those writing in business, self-help, or educational genres.

Pros:

- Professional Networking: Great for connecting with industry professionals, influencers, and potential collaborators.

- Content Credibility: Posts on LinkedIn are seen as more credible, particularly for professional and academic content.

Cons:

- Niche Audience: Not as effective for fiction authors or genres outside of business, education, and self-help.
- Lower Engagement: Engagement rates can be lower than on more casual social platforms.
- Best For: Nonfiction authors or those writing in genres related to business, leadership, or professional development.

Hashtags: Hashtags are useful on LinkedIn for increasing the reach of posts. Popular hashtags include #Leadership, #Business, #WritingCommunity, and #BookLaunch. As with other platforms, it's important to research which hashtags are currently active and relevant to your content.

Leveraging the appropriate social media platforms is crucial for authors' ongoing book marketing, as it ensures that you are effectively reaching the readers who are most likely to engage with your work. The key to success lies in finding the balance between where your readers hang out and where you feel comfortable—or can become comfortable—engaging with them.

By focusing on platforms that align with your audience's habits and your own strengths, you can create meaningful, authentic interactions that drive interest and build loyalty over time. Whether it's Instagram for visual storytelling, Threads for conversation, or Facebook for community-building, being present and active in the right spaces will sustain your book's visibility and success.

CONTENT IDEAS

As authors, we all love to talk about our books, but it can be challenging to find the right words beyond just shouting, "buy, buy, buy!" It's important to engage your readers in ways that go beyond promotion, drawing them into the world of your book and your journey as a writer.

In this chapter, we'll explore a variety of content ideas that allow you to connect meaningfully with your audience—without sounding like a constant sales pitch. From behind-the-scenes insights and character spotlights to personal anecdotes and related book recommendations, this section will help you share your story in a way that deepens your relationship with readers and keeps them coming back for more.

TWENTY WAYS TO SHARE

Here are twenty ways you can engage your readers on social media and your newsletter that won't make you an "ask-hole":

1. What inspired you to start writing?

2. What is the key message of your book?
3. Who did you write this book for (your ideal reader)?
4. Where do you write?
5. What are your writing rituals?
6. Sneak peeks
7. Quotes from your book
8. Share about sending your book to your editor
9. Cover reveal
10. Facts about your book
11. Your book's themes
12. Photos or illustrations from the book
13. Video of you unboxing your book/seeing it for the first time
14. Early endorsements/advanced praise
15. Foreword writer announcement
16. Countdown to publication
17. About your publishing experience
18. Your biggest takeaway from the writing-publishing process
19. Celebrate launch day
20. Thank you for supporting you

GENERAL CONTENT

You can create many of these ahead and have them on-hand for sharing. I personally love inspirational quotes and have thousands of them curated. If you're a guest on someone's podcast, share the link to the interview.

- Inspirational quotes
- Facts, figures, and trivia
- Newsworthy updates
- Podcast interviews

- Television references
- Why your subject is important
- Your big WHY
- Relevant and/or related articles
- National holidays or awareness days

SUPPORT OTHER AUTHORS

In addition to highlighting your work and process, sharing what you're reading, spotlighting other authors, and putting good juju into the Universe are also key. Here are a few ideas to get those creative juices flowing:

- Post about your favorite author or book
- Share a photo of your To-Be-Read pile
- Share a post from your favorite bookshop
- Take a picture of your favorite reading nook
- Show your bookshelves
- Provide a review of a book you've read

CURATED CONTENT FROM OTHER SOURCES

When it comes to engaging with your audience, you don't have to create every piece of content yourself. In fact, curating valuable content from other sources is a great way to keep your readers informed, inspired, and engaged. Whether it's sharing an article from an industry leader, recommending a fellow author's work, or posting relevant news, curating content shows that you're in touch with your community and enhances your brand without the pressure of constant creation. Curation allows you to provide value while broadening the conversation beyond your own voice. So, where does one find items to curate? Here are a few sources where you can find appropriate curated content:

- Google alerts
- Reddit
- Blog posts
- Magazine articles
- Industry influencers
- Regular news outlets
- Twitter and LinkedIn

As you've seen throughout this chapter, countless ways exist to engage your readers beyond just promoting your book. By offering a variety of content—behind-the-scenes glimpses, personal stories, or recommendations—you create a richer, more dynamic connection with your audience.

Remember, the key to building lasting relationships with your readers is to offer value, spark curiosity, and keep the conversation going. With these content ideas, you now have a toolkit to keep your readers engaged, excited, and eagerly anticipating what comes next in your writing journey.

YOUR EMAIL LIST

An email list is an author's *most valuable asset*—more crucial than social media followers because you own your email list. It lets you communicate directly with your audience, share updates, and promote new releases. Offer a lead magnet, such as a free chapter or exclusive content, to encourage visitors to subscribe. Regularly send newsletters to keep your subscribers engaged and informed. An entire chapter of this book is dedicated to building your list and sending regular communications.

CREATE VALUABLE CONTENT

It is essential to produce and share content that resonates with your audience regularly. This can include blog posts, articles, podcasts, videos, or even social media posts. Focus on topics that are relevant to your readers and that showcase your expertise and personality. Consistency is critical to keeping your audience engaged and growing your platform.

ENGAGE WITH YOUR AUDIENCE

Building an author platform isn't just about broadcasting your message; it's about creating a community. Engage with your audience by responding to comments, asking for feedback, and creating opportunities for interaction. This helps build loyalty and trust, making your readers more likely to support your work.

For introverted authors, interacting with an audience can feel challenging, but there are several ways to connect that align with a more reserved or introspective nature:

- **Start a Blog**. Blogging allows you to share your thoughts, insights, and experiences in a controlled environment. You can write at your own pace and publish content that resonates with your audience without the need for real-time interaction. Your blog posts can offer behind-the-scenes looks at your writing process, reflections on themes in your books, or even book recommendations.
- **Utilize Social Media.** Thoughtfully: Platforms like Instagram or Twitter can be used in a way that feels less overwhelming. For instance, you can schedule posts ahead of time or share curated content like inspirational quotes, book excerpts, or photos of your workspace. Engagement doesn't always have to be instantaneous; you can respond to comments and messages at your own comfort level.
- **Engage through Newsletters**. Sending out a monthly or quarterly newsletter is a great way to connect with readers. In your newsletter, you can share updates on your writing, personal anecdotes, book recommendations, or even exclusive content

like short stories or first looks at new work. This method allows you to interact with your audience on your terms, with no pressure for immediate interaction.

GROWING YOUR LIST

Growing your author email list is essential for building a dedicated readership and boosting book sales. There are several effective ways to expand your list:

- **Offer a Freebie.** This incentive could be a downloadable short story, bonus chapter, autographed bookplate, bookmarks, coloring sheets, or writing tips, in exchange for signing up. Promote this lead magnet on your website, social media, and during virtual events.
- **Calls-to-Action.** Include a call-to-action (CTA) on blog posts or guest articles, encouraging readers to subscribe for exclusive updates.
- **Cross-Promote.** Partnering with other authors or business owners for cross-promotions or giveaways can introduce you to new readers.
- **Leverage Live Events.** Promoting your newsletter at live events, interviews, book signings, or in your books' back matter can help convert readers into subscribers, ensuring you build relationships with your audience.
- **Ask.** Get in the habit of ending interactions or calls by asking if the person you're talking to might be interested in your newsletter. Be prepared to tell them why they might enjoy reading it.

Caution: Under NO circumstances is it okay to add people to your email list without their permission.

UTILIZE SEO AND ANALYTICS

Understanding search engine optimization (SEO) can help increase the visibility of your website and content (this is also why I highly recommend using a Wordpress.org website). Use relevant keywords, meta descriptions, and tags to optimize your site for search engines.

Additionally, use analytics tools to track your audience's behavior and preferences. This can inform your content strategy and help you make data-driven decisions. Working with a professional can elevate and enhance your visibility and reach in this area.

OTHER WAYS TO
BUILD YOUR PLATFORM

I n addition to creating a website, leveraging social media, and building an email list, several other effective ways to build your author platform exist, such as:

- **Guest Blog.** Guest blogging on popular blogs or websites in your genre can help you reach new audiences and establish yourself as an authority in your field.
- **Podcast.** Podcasting is another powerful tool; whether you start your own podcast or appear as a guest on others, it allows you to share your insights, connect with listeners, and promote your work in a more personal and engaging format.
- **Speak.** Speaking engagements—whether at conferences, book fairs, or online webinars— provide opportunities to showcase your expertise and connect directly with potential readers.
- **Collaborate.** Collaborating with other authors on joint projects, anthologies, or cross-promotions

can help you tap into each other's audiences and expand your reach.

These strategies, when combined with consistent engagement and quality content, can significantly enhance your author platform and contribute to long-term success.

NETWORK WITH OTHER WRITERS AND INDUSTRY PROFESSIONALS

Networking is key to expanding your reach and credibility. Connect with other authors, publishers, bloggers, and influencers in your genre. Attend writing conferences, participate in online writing communities, and collaborate on projects. Building relationships within the industry can open doors to new opportunities and help you grow your platform. Writing can be a lonely business, but being a successful author requires a community.

Take time to find a networking organization that aligns with your goals and personality—not all networking organizations are the same. Look for one that champions authors and includes other bookish professionals, such as publishers, editors, graphic designers, marketing experts, and book coaches.

Ninja tip: Book virtual or in-person coffee dates with people you meet to get to know them better and they you.

OBTAINING AND USING
SOCIAL PROOF

REVIEWS, ENDORSEMENTS, AND BLURBS, OH MY!

Book reviews, endorsements, and blurbs are critical tools in an author's marketing arsenal, serving as powerful social proof that can significantly influence potential readers' purchasing decisions. Books with a high number of reviews attract more attention and tend to rank higher on platforms like Amazon, increasing their visibility.

According to a study by BookBub, books with over 150 reviews see a more than fourfold increase in sales compared to those with fewer reviews.

Similarly, Goodreads reports that books with more than 1,000 ratings are 97% more likely to be included in recommendation lists, further boosting their discoverability. These statistics underscore the importance of actively seeking and promoting reviews and endorsements to enhance your book's credibility and reach.

REVIEWS

Book reviews are evaluations of your book written by readers, critics, or bloggers, often posted on platforms like Amazon,

Goodreads, or personal blogs. Reviews offer potential readers insights into the book's quality, themes, and appeal, serving as social proof that can influence purchasing decisions.

The quantity and quality of reviews can affect a book's visibility in online stores, as algorithms favor titles with more engagement. Reviews are essential because they provide honest, peer-based evaluations that can attract more readers and build trust in your work.

ENDORSEMENTS

Endorsements are positive statements about your book typically provided by established authors, experts, or celebrities in your genre. These endorsements are usually found on the book's cover or the front pages. Endorsements lend credibility and prestige to your book, as readers often trust recommendations from recognized figures. A strong endorsement can significantly impact a reader's decision to purchase a book, particularly if the endorser is well-respected.

BLURBS

Advanced reader blurbs are similar to endorsements but are specifically given by early readers, such as those who receive an Advance Reader Copy (ARC) before the book's official release. These blurbs can be used in marketing materials, the book's cover, or online descriptions. Advanced reader blurbs are crucial because they create early buzz around your book and can generate initial reviews even before the book is officially launched.

WHY YOU WANT ALL THREE

While reviews are generally more detailed and come from a broad audience, endorsements, and blurbs are typically shorter and come from specific, often influential, individuals. Reviews provide a wide range of opinions that help other readers gauge the book's general reception. Endorsements offer targeted, high-impact praise that can lend your book instant credibility. Advanced reader blurbs combine the benefits of both, offering early validation that can drive pre-orders and initial sales.

These elements work together to create a robust marketing strategy. Reviews offer a broad base of social proof, endorsements provide authoritative credibility, and advanced reader blurbs generate early excitement and buzz, all contributing to your book's overall success and visibility.

Note: For the remainder of this section, we will use the term "reviews" to encompass reviews, endorsements, and blurbs collectively. This will simplify the discussion while acknowledging the distinct but related roles these forms of feedback play in book promotion.

GETTING REVIEWS

The advance reader (ARC) process to obtain blurbs happens after your book has been completely edited and laid out but before proofreading (typically, these happen concurrently).

Typically, your publisher will manage the book blurb process, but you also have a role in finding ARC readers within your community. You'll first ask permission, then either follow these steps yourself or provide your publisher with names and email addresses so she can contact them directly.

Reach out via email (or FB messenger or Instagram direct message) to inquire about their interest and availability to read and review your book. Include the following:

- Your book summary (a short paragraph describing your book)
- The total number of pages you're asking them to read (could be the full manuscript or an excerpt)
- What date you need their review by

- Tell them how you'll use their review (back cover copy, interior "Advanced Praise" section, and in marketing copy)

When someone says "yes," celebrate! Then follow up by sending them the following information via email (gently remind them that you're not looking for editing or proof-reading comments):

- Your manuscript or excerpt (PDF only)
- How you want them to send you the review (email, FB messenger, text)
- What date you need their review by
- Ask if they would also be willing to post a review on Amazon once your book goes live. They should use the following language, "I received an Advanced Reader Copy of the book from the author, and this review is my opinion of said book."

If someone says "no," celebrate! Their refusal has nothing to do with you—be grateful they closed the loop.

Thank your potential reviewers and those who provided a blurb. Consider offering a free copy of your print or ebook as a concrete way of saying, "Thank you for taking the time to read my book and offer a blurb."

WHY REVIEWS MATTER

Book reviews are critical for your book's success. They provide social proof to potential readers and play a key role in boosting your book's visibility on platforms like Amazon and Goodreads. The more reviews you have, the more likely your book will appear in search results, recommendations, and promotions, leading to increased sales and readership.

Book reviews play a crucial role in the longevity and success of a book. Statistics show that books with a higher number of reviews not only gain more visibility but also have a longer sales lifespan. For instance, books with more than 150 reviews significantly increase sales compared to those with fewer reviews, often boosting sales by up to 4.5 times.[13] This increased visibility is due to algorithms on platforms like Amazon, which favor books with more reviews, pushing them higher in search results and recommendations.[14]

Moreover, the average book sells around 200 copies in its first year, but this number can rise significantly with a strong review presence, potentially reaching 1,000 copies over its lifetime[11]. This demonstrates that actively seeking and accumulating reviews can significantly extend a book's market presence and enhance its long-term success.

Ninja Tip: Giving reviews generously creates goodwill among other authors, who are likely to also share your books with their readers. Get in the habit of writing and posting reviews of books you've read.

Securing reviews is not just about initial sales but about sustaining your book's relevance and visibility in a competitive market over time.

WHERE ELSE TO GET REVIEWS

- **Amazon:** The most influential platform for

reviews. Reviews here directly impact your book's ranking and visibility.

- **Goodreads:** A hub for book lovers, where reviews can help build credibility and connect with a community of readers. https://www.goodreads.com/
- **StoryGraph:** This is an excellent non-Amazon alternative to Goodreads. https://www.thestorygraph.com/
- **LibraryThing:** An engaged group of readers, who enter a lottery to win the chance to read and review your book. If they win, they are obligated to provide a review on LibraryThing. As the author, you determine how many of your books to include in the giveaway, and your publisher sets it up within LibraryThing. This is a fantastic way to interact with potential fans—you can include a thank you note and flat SWAG with your book to readers. https://www.librarything.com/
- **Book Blogs**: Reach out to bloggers who specialize in your genre. A positive review from a well-regarded blog can drive significant interest.
- **Social Media:** Encourage readers to share their thoughts on platforms like Instagram, Twitter, and Facebook, where their networks can see their recommendations. Be sure to ask them to tag you so you can see (and share) their reviews.
- **Book Clubs and Reader Communities:** Engage with book clubs and online reading communities. These groups often post reviews and discuss books in detail.

HOW TO ASK FOR REVIEWS

When asking for reviews, being polite, clear, and respectful of your readers' time is important. Here are some tips:

- **Be Direct, But Not Pushy:** Make it clear that reviews are valuable to you but avoid making the reader feel pressured.
- **Personalize Your Request**: If you're emailing or messaging individual readers, personalize your request to show you value their opinion.
- **Provide Easy Instructions:** Include direct links to where they can leave a review to make the process as simple as possible.
- **Express Gratitude**: Always thank your readers for their support, whether or not they choose to leave a review.

HOW OFTEN TO ASK FOR REVIEWS

- **Immediately After Purchase:** Prompt readers to leave a review shortly after they purchase or finish your book. This is when the experience is freshest in their minds.
- **During Promotional Campaigns:** If you're running a discount or giveaway, ask readers to leave a review in exchange for a free or discounted copy.
- **Post-Event:** Remind attendees to leave a review after virtual or in-person events like book signings or readings.
- **Regularly on Social Media:** Periodically remind your followers to leave a review, especially when you hit milestones (like 100 reviews).

- **Ongoing in Your Newsletter:** Include a review link to one review site in every email, reminding readers how crucial their reviews are.

EMAIL SCRIPT FOR REQUESTING REVIEWS

Here's a simple, effective email script you can use to ask for reviews:

Subject: A Quick Favor for [Your Book Title]

Hi [Reader's Name],

I hope this message finds you well! I wanted to take a moment to thank you for reading [Your Book Title]. It means the world to me that you took the time to dive into my work.

If you enjoyed the book, I would be incredibly grateful if you could take a few minutes to leave a review on [Amazon/Goodreads/Other Platform]. Your feedback not only helps other readers discover the book but also supports my journey as an author.

Here's the link to leave your review: [Insert Link]

Thank you so much for your support—I truly appreciate it!

Best wishes,
[Your Name]

TIPS FOR REVIEWERS

As a believer in karma, I feel that one must write and publish reviews to receive them. Follow these tips to write effective and helpful reviews for the books you read. You can also incorporate these tips into your email requesting reviews.

- Don't be fancy—write in short, easy-to-read sentences.
- Start with facts about the book—offer review readers clarity on what you'll cover.
- Avoid spoilers (or alert readers for potential spoilers).
- Offer comparisons (e.g., If you enjoyed X, you'll enjoy Y).
- Say what you loved and what you wanted that wasn't there.
- Put yourself in other readers' shoes: what would you have wanted to know before you picked up this book?

ADDITIONAL TIPS FOR GATHERING REVIEWS

- **Follow-up:** If someone mentioned they enjoyed your book but has yet to leave a review, follow up with a gentle reminder.
- **Offer Incentives:** While you can't directly offer rewards for reviews on platforms like Amazon, you can offer incentives like entry into a giveaway for those who post honest reviews.
- **Engage with Reviewers:** Thank reviewers personally and engage with them on social media.

This builds a relationship and encourages future reviews.

Ninja Tip: If someone tells you how much they enjoyed your book, jot down their verbal review, write it up, and send it to them with a note that you hope it's okay that you drafted a review for them to post. Tell them to feel free to edit the review before posting.

By strategically asking for reviews and making the process as easy as possible for your readers, you can significantly increase the number of reviews for your book, boosting its visibility and success.

HOW TO USE REVIEWS

Book reviews, endorsements, and blurbs are more than just feedback from readers; they are powerful tools that can be strategically leveraged to enhance your book's visibility, credibility, and sales. Whether you're a new author or a seasoned writer, knowing how to effectively use reviews can significantly impact your marketing efforts. This section explores various ways to utilize book reviews to maximize their impact, from boosting your online presence to incorporating them into your promotional materials.

HIGHLIGHT REVIEWS ON YOUR WEBSITE

- **Why It Matters**: Featuring positive reviews on your website adds credibility and can persuade potential readers to purchase your book. Create a dedicated section for testimonials or feature quotes on your homepage to showcase the praise your book has received.

- **How to Do It**: Select the most impactful excerpts from reviews and display them prominently on your site. If possible, include the reviewer's name and the source to enhance authenticity.

USE REVIEWS IN SOCIAL MEDIA MARKETING

- **Why It Matters**: Social media platforms are excellent for sharing book reviews with a wider audience. Posting excerpts from reviews can generate interest and encourage your followers to check out your book.
- **How to Do It**: Share snippets of glowing reviews on platforms like Instagram, Twitter, and Facebook. Accompany the quotes with a call-to-action, such as a link to purchase the book or a prompt to leave their own review.

Ninja Tip: Using Canva, create a "testimonial" template, duplicate it, update the reviews, and download it. Save all the testimonial images to a digital file to use as part of your overall social media strategy.

INCORPORATE REVIEWS INTO YOUR BOOK'S DESCRIPTION

- **Why It Matters**: Including reviews in your book's product description on sites like Amazon or Goodreads can immediately provide potential buyers with social proof of your book's quality.

- **How to Do It**: Add a few standout quotes from professional reviewers or enthusiastic readers to the top of your book's description. Ensure these reviews are concise and impactful, highlighting key aspects of your book that appeal to readers. Your publisher ought to do this when uploading your book files to the various publishing sites.

LEVERAGE REVIEWS IN EMAIL CAMPAIGNS

- **Why It Matters**: Email marketing is a direct way to reach potential readers and including positive reviews can increase engagement and conversion rates.
- **How to Do It**: When sending newsletters or promotional emails, include a short review snippet alongside information about your book. This builds interest and provides social proof that can encourage purchases.

INCLUDE REVIEWS IN PRINT MATERIALS

- **Why It Matters**: Reviews can also be effectively used in physical marketing materials like bookmarks, postcards, or flyers, especially during book launches or signings.
- **How to Do It**: Print excerpts of the best reviews on promotional materials you distribute at events or include with purchases. This tangible endorsement can reinforce your book's appeal.

PITCH MEDIA OUTLETS USING REVIEWS

- **Why It Matters**: When reaching out to media outlets, bloggers, or influencers for additional coverage, including positive reviews can strengthen your pitch and increase the likelihood of being featured.
- **How to Do It**: Attach a press kit with a summary of the best reviews and your pitch. Highlighting strong reviews can help convince media contacts that your book is worth their attention.

USE REVIEWS IN ADVERTISING

- **Why It Matters**: Advertisements featuring compelling reviews can enhance the credibility of your book and increase click-through rates.
- **How to Do It**: Incorporate short, positive quotes from reviews into your online ads, such as Facebook ads or Google ads. Highlighting a reviewer's praise in your ad copy can draw attention and persuade potential readers to learn more.

Note: Paid advertising can be a waste of marketing resources. People discover books through various channels, with some being more influential than others.

According to a Penguin Random House study, word of mouth remains the most powerful method, influencing around 49% of readers' decisions. Online retailers like Amazon are also significant, with around 26% of readers discovering books this way. Social media is increasingly important, especially among younger demographics, impacting about 20% of readers. Book reviews and recommendations from trusted sources also play a key role in guiding readers' choices.[12]

You'll notice that "paid advertising" is not a top way for people to discover your books. By strategically using book reviews across various platforms and marketing channels, you can amplify their impact, enhancing your book's reputation and driving sales. Reviews serve as powerful endorsements that, when used effectively, can help you reach a broader audience and build lasting success.

HOW TO GET BOOK REVIEWS FROM PUBLICATIONS

1. Send out review copies of your book. Lots of them. More than you think you ought to.
2. Send ARCs and your EPK to every major newspaper and magazine that might be interested in your book's subject.
3. For every 100 copies you send out, you get 200 orders—a pretty great return on investment (ROI).
4. Budget five-to-ten per cent of your first printing as giveaways—for reviewers, booksellers, and key opinion makers.

Here is a list of potential nonfiction book reviewers to whom you could send an advanced reader copy (ARC) or your book after publication, along with your electronic press kit.

- ***Publishers Weekly***: http://www.bookmarket.com/ pw.html

- **Kirkus Reviews**: Sarah Gold (nonfiction), 200 Park Avenue South #1118, New York, NY 10003-1543.
- **Booklist**: Mary Ellen Quinn, Booklist, American Library Association, 50 E. Huron St., Chicago, IL 60611-2729 or www.ala.org/booklist (two copies needed).
- **Choice**: Book Review Editor, *Choice*, 100 Riverview Center, Middletown, CT 06457 OR email submissions@ala-choice.org (they review finished books only).
- **Washington Post Book World**: Nina King, Editor, *Washington Post Book World*, 1150 15th Street NW, Washington, DC 20071 (http://www. washingtonpost.com).
- **San Francisco Chronicle Book Review**: Patricia Holt, Review Editor, *San Francisco Chronicle*, 275 Fifth Street, San Francisco, CA 94103 OR email: patholt@sfgate.com.
- **Los Angeles Times Book Review**: Steve Wasserman, Book Review Editor, *Los Angeles Times Book Review*, Times Mirror Square, Los Angeles, CA 90053.
- **Chicago Tribune Books**: Elizabeth Taylor, Book Review Editor, *Chicago Tribune Books*, 435 N. Michigan Avenue, Room 400, Chicago, IL 66011-4022.
- **USA Today**: Deirdre Donohue, Book Review Editor, *USA Today*, 1000 Wilson Blvd., Arlington, VA 22229
- **New York Review of Books**: Robert B. Silvers or Barbara Epstein, Editors, *New York Review of Books*, 1755 Broadway, 5th Floor, New York, NY 10019.

- ***Midwest Book Review***: James Cox, Midwest Book Review, 278 Orchard Drive, Oregon, Wisconsin 53575

Note: Read and follow each publication's submission guidelines. Some require paperback copies, others take PDF copies, and others want eBook copies. Double-check mailing addresses as these sometimes change.

BOOK TOURS AND EVENTS

BOOK CLUBS, BOOKSTORES, AND LIBRARIES

Book clubs, bookstores, and libraries are essential allies in an author's post-publishing success. These communities provide valuable platforms for promoting your book, engaging with readers, and driving long-term sales. Book clubs create opportunities for deeper discussion and word-of-mouth marketing, while bookstores offer in-person exposure through events and displays. Libraries play a crucial role in expanding your book's reach, offering it to a broad audience while often hosting author talks and signings. Together, these channels provide sustained visibility, foster loyal readership, and help authors build lasting relationships with readers. Before we dig into the "how" of finding and securing reading events, let's first explore how to prepare for them.

BOOK CLUBS

Book clubs offer authors an incredible opportunity to connect directly with readers in meaningful ways and extend the life of their book. There are many kinds of book clubs, from local community groups that meet in libraries or homes to virtual clubs on platforms like Facebook and Goodreads. Some clubs are genre-specific, while others focus on general fiction, non-fiction, or even niche topics like memoirs or historical fiction.

Authors can find these clubs through social media, local libraries, independent bookstores, or online platforms like Meetup and Bookclubs.com. Participating in or engaging with these groups can lead to word-of-mouth promotion and valuable feedback from dedicated readers. Here are some best practices for discovering book clubs:

- Ask friends who love to read if they belong to any book clubs
- Visit your local library and inquire about their book clubs
- Discover your local independent bookstores and see if they have any book clubs

BOOK STORES

Independent bookstores are vital hubs for local communities and play a crucial role in supporting authors and fostering literary culture. Unlike large chains, indie bookstores often offer personalized recommendations, host book signings and events, and actively promote the works of emerging authors. They're also known for cultivating loyal customer bases who value unique, curated selections.

Authors can use resources like Bookshop (https://www.bookshop.org), IndieBound (https://www.indiebound.org/), the American Booksellers Association website (https://www.bookweb.org/), or social media groups dedicated to book lovers to find independent bookstores. Visiting and engaging with these bookstores can help authors build strong relation-ships and create lasting connections with readers.

BUILD RELATIONSHIPS WITH INDIE BOOKSTORES

- Find them on social media and follow them. Make a habit of commenting on their posts and attending virtual events that appeal to you.
- If you feel comfortable, visit your local independent bookstores. If you need help, you can always connect via email.
- Identify other local authors, connect with them, and consider proposing a joint event at your local bookstores.

Here's a sample email you can use to contact bookstores near you:

Dear [Owner or Acquisitions Professional],

As a long-time patron of [insert bookstore name] and local author, I wanted to introduce myself and share the news that my book, [*title*], will be published on [date]. It will be available in both print and digital forms for you to put on your online bookstore or via purchase for your bookshelves. I'm attaching my media guide, which has all the information on the content of my book and information for accessing it.

I'm available via [how to contact you] for any questions.

Thank you!

[your signature block]

LIBRARIES

Engaging with local libraries is an important step for authors looking to build strong community support and expand their reach. Librarians love championing local authors, often showcasing their books, hosting events, and recommending their work to patrons. By connecting with your local library, you're tapping into a trusted, community-centered space that can introduce your book to a broad, engaged audience.

Libraries often hold author talks, readings, and book signings, which boost visibility and foster meaningful relationships with readers and librarians alike. For authors, libraries are not just places to house books, but vibrant hubs for building lasting local support.

To locate your local library acquisitions contact, visit https://search.worldcat.org/libraries. (Note: this link presently only works for libraries located in the U.S.) Remember also to contact your hometown, high school, and college library systems!

Here's a sample email template you can use to contact your librarians:

Dear [Acquisitions Librarian's first name],

As a long-time patron of [insert library name] and local author, I wanted to introduce myself and share the news that my book, [*title*], will publish on [date]. It will be available in both print and digital forms for your purchase or via a cost-per-check-out model (for the digital version). I'm attaching my media guide, which has all the information on the content of my book as well as information for accessing it.

I'm available via [how to contact you] for any questions you may have.

Thank you!
[your signature block]

_____

.

WHY CONSIDER BOOK
TOURS AND EVENTS?

Book tours and events are invaluable opportunities for authors to connect with readers, build their brand, and boost book sales. These events allow for direct interaction, where authors can share their stories, discuss their work, and build a loyal readership. In-person events, such as signings, readings, and workshops, create memorable experiences that can deepen the connection with your audience. Virtual book tours, on the other hand, offer the flexibility to reach a broader audience without geographical limitations.

Ninja Tip: Leverage the word "and" in your marketing efforts. Do virtual events AND live ones.

Authors should consider book tours and events as powerful tools for connecting with their audience, building their brand, and driving book sales. These events offer unique opportunities for personal interaction, allowing readers to engage with the author beyond the pages of their books. Whether in-person or virtual, book events can generate buzz, attract media attention, and create memorable experiences that foster a loyal readership. By stepping out and directly engaging with readers, authors can significantly enhance their visibility and strengthen their connection with their audience. Additionally, consider these benefits:

- **Personal Connection**: Engaging directly with readers creates a personal bond, making them more likely to support your work and spread the word.
- **Increased Visibility:** Events generate buzz and can attract media coverage, which helps reach new readers.
- **Sales Boost:** Events often lead to immediate book sales, as attendees are typically eager to purchase a signed copy or a book they've just heard about.

EFFECTIVE WAYS TO EXECUTE A BOOK TOUR OR EVENT

- **Collaborate with Local Bookstores**: Partner with local bookstores for signings and readings. These venues often have loyal customers and can help promote the event. Independent bookstores are often more supportive of lesser-known and local authors than the big box stores.
- **Utilize Virtual Platforms:** Host online events via Zoom or social media live streams to engage with readers worldwide. Virtual events are cost-

effective and can be recorded for future marketing purposes.

- **Engage with Book Clubs:** Contact book clubs to host discussions or Q&A sessions in person or virtually. This allows for a deeper dive into your book and creates a dedicated community of readers.
- **Cross-Promote with Other Authors:** Team up with other authors for joint events to draw in a larger crowd and introduce your book to new audiences.

Whether in-person or virtual, book tours and events are essential strategies for building your author brand and driving book sales.

PLANNING A BOOK TOUR

P lanning a book tour is an exciting yet complex process that can significantly boost your book's visibility and connect you with readers. A well-executed tour involves careful planning, from selecting the right venues to coordinating logistics and promoting the events. Whether you're an established author or launching your first book, organizing a successful tour requires a strategic approach to ensure each stop maximizes impact.

This section will walk you through the essential steps, best practices, and common pitfalls to avoid when planning a book tour, helping you make the most of this valuable promotional opportunity.

BEST PRACTICES

- **Start Early:** Begin planning your book tour at least six-to-nine months in advance to secure venues, organize logistics, and coordinate promotion.

- **Research Venues:** Choose locations where your target audience is most likely to attend. Consider bookstores, libraries, community centers, and relevant conferences.
- **Coordinate with Local Media:** Reach out to local newspapers, radio stations, and bloggers to cover your event. Media exposure can significantly boost attendance and awareness. This is a great use for your electronic press kit!
- **Leverage Social Media:** Promote your tour across all social media platforms, using event pages, live updates, and interactive content to engage your audience.
- **Engage with Local Communities:** Connect with local book clubs, schools, or writing groups to participate in your events, either as co-hosts or attendees.

Ninja Tip: Start building relationships with local bookstores early, attend other events to see how they're run, and engage frequently with the store's event coordinator.

WHAT TO AVOID

- **Overextending:** Avoid planning too many stops too close together. Ensure you have adequate time to rest and travel between events to maintain energy and enthusiasm.
- **Ignoring Logistics:** Don't overlook the details like transportation, accommodations, and shipping

books to each venue. These logistical elements can
make or break your tour.

- **Poor Communication:** Keep all stakeholders
informed, including venue contacts, media
partners, and your audience. Clear communication
ensures everyone is on the same page and helps
avoid last-minute issues.
- **Neglecting Virtual Options:** In today's digital
world, consider integrating virtual events into your
tour to reach a broader audience.

By following these best practices and avoiding common
pitfalls, you can ensure a successful book tour that effectively
promotes your book and strengthens your connection with
readers.

BEST PRACTICES FOR
BOOK READINGS

By following these best practices, you can create a memorable, engaging reading experience that builds deeper connections with your readers, the community, and fosters long-term interest in your book:

Ninja Tip: Prepare a list of suggested questions for the moderator to use—these can come from your EPK!

- **Prepare an Engaging Excerpt:** Select a passage highlighting your book's themes, style, or unique characters. Aim for something short (five to ten minutes) to keep the audience's attention, ending on a cliffhanger or pivotal moment to spark curiosity.

Ninja Tip: If you're not starting your reading at the beginning of your book, be sure to give thought and preparation to grounding your listeners in the action—without spoilers!

- **Practice Your Delivery:** Read the excerpt aloud several times before the event to ensure smooth pacing and confidence. Focus on clear pronunciation, varying your tone for emphasis, and maintaining eye contact to engage the audience.
- **Know Your Audience:** Tailor your reading to suit the setting. If you're reading at a book club, expect a more informal discussion-based setting, whereas a bookstore or library may have a mixed audience, requiring a slightly broader appeal.
- **Create Interaction:** Encourage questions or discussion after the reading. Ask open-ended questions to stimulate conversation and connect with the audience, making the experience feel more personal.
- **Your Autograph:** Practice your autograph beforehand, ensuring that your autograph differs from your legal signature. Think of a way to sign the books that ties in with your book's theme. For example, Laura Pritchett signed her copy of *Three Keys* as "Stay Wild" along with her name.

Ninja Tip: Use either a black Ultra-Fine Sharpie or a Uniball pen for autographs. The extra benefit of using a Uniball pen is that it can't be counterfeited. *Fun Fact*: the Uniball pen was designed by Frank Abagnale, Jr., whose story was made in a Steven Spielberg biopic, *Catch Me if You Can.*

- **Bring Materials:** Have bookmarks, postcards, or signed copies of your book available for purchase. Providing a tangible takeaway can leave a lasting impression and increase sales.
- **Promote the Event:** Promote the reading beforehand via your newsletter, social media, and the venue's platforms. The more you promote, the more attendees you're likely to attract—and the more impactful and memorable your event will be.
- **Be Personable and Approachable:** Your personality can leave as strong an impression as your book. Smile, show enthusiasm, and thank the organizers and attendees for their time and support.
- **Send Thank You Notes:** Follow up your visit with a handwritten note of gratitude!

NURTURING YOUR READERS

EMAIL MARKETING AND NEWSLETTERS

Email marketing and newsletters are crucial for authors to build and maintain direct relationships with their readers. Unlike social media, which is often subject to algorithm changes, email provides a reliable, personal way to communicate directly with your audience. Newsletters allow you to share updates, exclusive content, and promotional offers, keeping your readers engaged and informed about your work. This consistent interaction strengthens reader loyalty, drives book sales, and supports long-term career growth by fostering a dedicated, engaged community.

Email marketing and newsletters are closely related but serve different purposes in an author's promotional strategy.

- **Email Marketing:** A broader strategy that encompasses all types of email communications sent to your audience, including promotional offers, sales announcements, event invitations, and updates about your books. Its primary goal is to drive specific actions, like purchasing a book or signing up for an event.

- **Newsletters:** A specific type of email content focused on providing regular, curated updates to your subscribers. Newsletters often include a mix of personal updates, upcoming events, exclusive content, and links to recent blog posts or media appearances. The goal is to build relationships with your readers and keep them engaged over time.

While email marketing is often more transactional, newsletters are relationship-building tools, fostering ongoing engagement with your audience.

Email marketing and newsletters are potent tools for authors to build strong, lasting connections with their readers. You can keep your readers engaged and informed by consistently delivering valuable content, updates, and exclusive offers directly to your audience's inbox. Whether announcing a new release, sharing behind-the-scenes insights, or offering special promotions, email is a personal and effective way to nurture your reader community. By planning your content, utilizing the right software, and maintaining a regular schedule, you can maximize the impact of your email marketing and newsletters, ultimately driving your success as an author.

EMAIL MARKETING

E mail marketing is vital for authors to engage with their readers and promote their work directly. This format is ideal for:

- Announcing new book releases
- Offering exclusive discounts
- Promoting upcoming events
- Sharing limited-time deals
- Special announcements like pre-orders
- Early access to new content

Best practices suggest sending marketing emails sparingly —typically no more than once or twice a month—to avoid overwhelming your subscribers while keeping them engaged and informed. Consistency, value-driven content, and clear calls-to-action are key to successful email marketing for authors.

CAN EMAIL MARKETING ITEMS BE ADDED TO A NEWSLETTER?

Whether to include book or event announcements in a newsletter or keep them separate depends on your audience and the content's frequency. If your newsletter already includes diverse content and your announcements fit naturally, it can be effective to combine them. This keeps your readers informed without overwhelming them with multiple emails. However, for significant announcements like a new book release or a major event, sending a dedicated email can help ensure the message stands out and receives the attention it deserves. Balancing these approaches is key to maintaining engagement without causing email fatigue.

HOW LONG SHOULD A MARKETING EMAIL BE?

An email marketing email should be concise and focused, typically between fifty and 200 words. The key is to convey your message clearly without overwhelming the reader. This length allows you to include essential details, such as a brief announcement, a call-to-action, and any necessary links while maintaining the reader's attention. Keep your email skimmable with short paragraphs, bullet points, or **bold text** for emphasis, ensuring that the main message is easily grasped at a glance.

BEST PRACTICES FOR EMAIL GRAPHICS

- **Keep It Simple**: Use clean, minimalistic designs that don't overwhelm the reader. Graphics should enhance, not overshadow, your message.

- **Optimize for Mobile**: Ensure graphics are responsive and look good on all devices. Mobile accounts for a significant portion of email opens.
- **Maintain Brand Consistency**: Use your brand's colors, fonts, and style in graphics to reinforce brand identity.
- **Include Alt Text**: Add descriptive alt text to graphics in case the images don't load.
- **Use Eye-Catching Images**: Choose high-quality visuals that draw attention and align with your content. DO NOT use images off the internet, as you could get into copyright troubles. Ensure that you have the appropriate licenses for use.
- **Limit File Size**: Keep images optimized for faster loading times without sacrificing quality.
- **Call-to-Action (CTA)**: Incorporate clear, clickable CTAs within your graphics, guiding readers on the next steps.

NEWSLETTERS

Author newsletters are a tool for building and maintaining a direct connection with your readers. Newsletters allow you to share updates, personal insights, exclusive content, and upcoming releases in a personalized way. Consistency is key to keeping your audience engaged; regular newsletters, whether weekly, monthly, or quarterly, ensure your readers remain interested in your journey. By providing valuable and timely content, you create a loyal readership that eagerly anticipates each update, ultimately driving deeper engagement and long-term success as an author. The key to consistently creating and publishing an impactful newsletter is following the KISS principle—keep it simple, silly! I suggest publishing your newsletter monthly on the same day of the month (for example, the first Sunday or the third Wednesday).

Cardinal rules for writing and publishing your newsletter:

1. Be consistent. Once you've established a rhythm with once a month, you can expand to twice a month or weekly.

2. Keep it simple and brief.
3. Include photos of your writing space, work-in-progress, garden, vacation, hobbies, bookshelves, and pets—especially your pets!
4. Show your personality—readers want to know YOU much more than they want to know your books.
5. Have FUN!

Here are additional ideas to include in your monthly author newsletter that incorporate photos:

- **Behind-the-Scenes**: Share images of your writing space, inspiration boards, or drafts in progress.
- **Character or Setting Visuals**: Showcase images that represent characters or settings from your book.
- **Bookstagram Style**: Feature aesthetically arranged photos of your books, including fan-submitted shots.
- **Author Life:** Include personal snapshots, such as attending events, speaking engagements, or traveling.
- **Exclusive Excerpts:** Pair a photo with a snippet from your upcoming book.
- **Fan Art or Reader Photos**: Share visuals from readers engaging with your book.

NEWSLETTER LAYOUT

Here's a simple newsletter layout that balances personal connection and event updates while highlighting your personality:

{Your Name's} Monthly Musings
Letter from the Author

A friendly, conversational note about your writing process, recent life events, or inspiration. (Insert a candid or relatable photo of yourself.)

Upcoming Events (or Publications)

{Event Name}: Date and time with a brief description.

{Event Name}: Date and time with RSVP or registration link. (Include event-related images or promotional banners.)

This Month's Highlight

A quirky, fun section showcasing something personal, like favorite books, writing tools, or a favorite hobby. (Add a playful or themed image.)

In the News

Highlight a review or something bookish that's grabbing the world by storm. You can also share your own reviews of other authors' work.

This layout is approachable and engaging and lets your personality shine through!

Ninja Tip: If you plan and write your newsletter first, you can leverage its contents for social media posts.

Email marketing and newsletters are potent tools for

authors to build strong, lasting connections with their readers. You can keep your readers engaged and informed by consistently delivering valuable content, updates, and exclusive offers directly to your audience's inbox. Whether announcing a new release, sharing behind-the-scenes insights, or offering special promotions, email is a personal and effective way to nurture your reader community. By planning your content, utilizing the right software, and maintaining a regular schedule, you can maximize the impact of your email marketing and newsletters, ultimately driving your success as an author.

PLANNING AND LEVERAGING THEMES

P lanning your author newsletter and social media content can ease the burden of consistency and provide valuable content to your readers. By organizing your themes in advance, you can ensure a steady flow of engaging updates without feeling rushed or overwhelmed. Each month can focus on a different aspect of your author journey or content that resonates with your audience.

Authors don't need to create all content from scratch; sharing information from other authors or publications can enrich newsletters and social media posts. Curating content like writing tips, book recommendations, or industry insights provides value and supports fellow writers.

For example, an author can share an insightful article on character development or recommend a book that influenced their writing style. This practice fosters a sense of community, saves time, and keeps content fresh. Associating with respected sources adds credibility to your platform. Always, always, always cite the author and publication!

Ninja Tip: Create an online file folder or use a Word document to snag articles and links that can be used throughout the year—kind of like a clipping file. When writing your newsletter, open the file and see what is relevant to your topic or theme.

MONTHLY NEWSLETTER THEME EXAMPLES

- **January**: New Year reflections and writing goals
- **February**: Behind the scenes of your writing process
- **March**: Book recommendations or influences
- **April**: Upcoming releases and teasers
- **May**: Q&A session with readers
- **June**: Favorite writing tools or tips
- **July**: Summer reading lists
- **August**: Character or setting spotlights
- **September**: Exclusive content, like short stories or excerpts
- **October**: Book club or reader group discussions
- **November**: Gratitude-themed updates or promotions
- **December**: Year-in-review and holiday greetings

You can also use the National Day and International Day calendars (https://www.nationaldaycalendar.com/ and https://www.nationaldaycalendar.com/international) for your newsletter and social media posts.

Ninja Tip: Create "Day of the Year" graphics once and reuse them annually.

This planned approach keeps your readers engaged and eagerly anticipating each newsletter, building loyalty and driving your long-term success. It also makes your life much easier!

EMAIL AND NEWSLETTER SOFTWARE

Choosing the right email marking and newsletter software is essential. The following are some popular tools that offer user-friendly interfaces and powerful features for authors:

- **Mailchimp**: Known for its ease of use and free tier, Mailchimp offers customizable templates, analytics, and audience segmentation, making it perfect for beginners and small mailing lists. To pre-schedule emails and newsletters for release, which I highly recommend, you'll need to purchase the inexpensive paid version. https://mailchimp.com/

- **MailerLite:** Offers simplicity and affordability with drag-and-drop editors, automation, and built-in surveys, perfect for authors who want streamlined features at a low cost. https://www.mailerlite.com/

- **ActiveCampaign:** A robust platform with advanced automation, personalization, and detailed reporting. Ideal for authors looking to scale their email marketing efforts. https://www.activecampaign.com/

Ninja Tip: Keep things simple. Start with an easy-to-use software and re-evaluate your needs annually. Most email software systems allow you to easily upload your existing email list from one platform to another.

IN CLOSING

As we end *Shelf Life: A Field Guide to Effective Post-Publishing Marketing*, it's important to reflect on the many strategies and tools that can help sustain your book's success long after its launch. From building a solid author platform and leveraging social media to securing book reviews and engaging with book clubs, bookstores, and libraries, each chapter has provided you with actionable steps to keep your book visible. We've explored how email marketing, newsletters, book tours, and events are powerful ways to connect directly with readers, while offering practical advice on using reviews and endorsements to enhance your credibility.

Marketing your book is not a sprint—it's a marathon. The reality is book sales can fluctuate, and overnight success is rare. But persistence is key. Consistently applying the marketing strategies discussed here will help you build a loyal readership and extend your book's reach. Even when you feel like the momentum has slowed, remember that every step contributes to the bigger picture, no matter how small.

Finally, take pride in your journey. Being an author is an

incredible accomplishment, and the process of sharing your work with the world, while challenging, is deeply rewarding. Keep experimenting, stay connected to your readers, and continue learning. Your story matters; with time and effort, you can ensure it finds its way to the right audience. Keep moving forward, one page at a time—your book's success is just the beginning of your journey as an author.

RESOURCES

AUTHOR WEBSITE

WordPress: https://wordpress.org/
Squarespace: https://www.squarespace.com/
Wix: https://www.wix.com/

EMAIL + NEWSLETTER SOFTWARE

Mailchimp: https://mailchimp.com/
MailerLite: https://www.mailerlite.com/
ActiveCampaign: https://www.activecampaign.com/

SOCIAL MEDIA

Canva (for graphics): https://www.canva.com/
Metricool (scheduler): https://metricool.com/
Social Sprout (scheduler): https://sproutsocial.com/

Planable (scheduler): https://planable.io/

FLAT SWAG

Bookmarks (2x6): https://www.nextdayflyers.com/
Stickers: https://stickerjunkie.com/
Bookplates (4x6): https://stickerjunkie.com/

MEDIA GUIDES

Create Your Electronic Press Kit (EPK): https://highlanderpressbooks.com/only-guide-you-need/
Book One Sheet Template (in Canva): https://www.canva.com/design/DAGRO7HPATE/MtGdUaDElAs68APHyQ-1OA/edit?utm_content=DAGRO7HPATE&utm_campaign=designshare&utm_medium=link2&utm_source=sharebutton

ENDNOTES

1. Tucker, Max. "Everything You Need to Know about Book Sales Figures." Scribe Media. Accessed September 19, 2024. https://scribemedia.com/book-sales/.

2. Thea. "Average Book Sales Figures: A Transparent Look into Publishing." Jericho Writers, March 8, 2023. https://jerichowriters.com/average-book-sales-figures/.

3. "Justice Department Sues to Block Penguin Random House Acquisition of S&S." PublishersWeekly.com, November 2, 2021. https://www.publishersweekly.com/pw/by-topic/industry-news/publisher-news/article/87783-doj-sues-to-block-prh-acquisition-of-s-s.html.

4. Tucker, Max. "Everything You Need to Know about Book Sales Figures." Scribe Media. Accessed September 19, 2024. https://scribemedia.com/book-sales/.

5. Tucker, Max. "Everything You Need to Know about Book Sales Figures." Scribe Media. Accessed September 19, 2024. https://scribemedia.com/book-sales/.

6. Rizzo, Nicholas. "Nicholas Rizzo." WordsRated, November 20, 2023. https://wordsrated.com/self-published-book-sales-statistics/.

7. Williams, Terry. "The Complete Guide to Amazon Book Sales: Statistics, Trends and Insights for 2024." 33rd Square, October 22, 2023. https://www.33rdsquare.com/the-complete-guide-to-amazon-book-sales-statistics-trends-and-insights-for-2023/.

8. "Global Social Media Statistics - DataReportal – Global Digital Insights." DataReportal. Accessed September 19, 2024. https://datareportal.com/social-media-users.

9. "Threads Revenue and Usage Statistics (2024)." Business of Apps, July 8, 2024. https://www.businessofapps.com/data/threads-statistics/.

10. "Tiktok Statistics You Need to Know in 2024." Backlinko, July 1, 2024. https://backlinko.com/tiktok-users.

11. Saxena, Esha. "27 Important Book Sales Statistics to Know (2024 Data)." GrabOn Blog - Powered by GrabOn.com, September 16, 2024. https://grabon.com/blog/book-sales-statistics/.

12. "News for Authors." Random Notes. Accessed September 19, 2024. https://authornews.penguinrandomhouse.com/trends-in-book-discovery-infographic/.

13. Williams, Terry. "The Complete Guide to Amazon Book Sales: Statistics, Trends and Insights for 2024." 33rd Square, October 22, 2023. https://www.33rdsquare.com/the-complete-guide-to-amazon-book-sales-statistics-trends-and-insights-for-2023/.

14. Williams, Terry. "The Complete Guide to Amazon Book Sales: Statistics, Trends and Insights for 2024." 33rd Square, October 22, 2023. https://www.33rdsquare.com/the-complete-guide-to-amazon-book-sales-statistics-trends-and-insights-for-2023/.

ACKNOWLEDGMENTS

This book would not exist without the incredible support, inspiration, and encouragement from so many amazing people in my life.

To **Dan Manzanares**, whose thoughtful feedback on my *Shelf Life* presentation to Western Colorado University's alumni of the Graduate Program in Creative Writing inspired me to write this book. To the alumni who attended my talk and found it helpful—thank you for your enthusiasm and engagement. Your support planted the seeds for this work.

To **Hanne Broter**, who not only created this gorgeous cover, she designed my personal brand and that of Highlander Press. She's an incredible artist, musician, and an even better friend.

To my **Faith Keepers Mastermind group**—Jill, Nicole, Carrie, Clare, and Jen—you keep me focused and energized, always encouraging me to share my wisdom. Your unwavering belief in me picks me up when the doldrums hit, and I'm so grateful for your friendship and insight.

To my early readers—**Lorraine, Kris, Mark, Rob, Jennia, and Maribeth**—thank you for taking the time to read, share your thoughtful feedback, and write your beautiful blurbs. Your encouragement and insight made this book stronger.

To the **Highlander Press authors** I've had the privilege to work with, thank you for the gift of your questions and for trusting me as your editor and publisher. I learn so much from each of you, and your wisdom, kindness, and love inspire me daily. Keep creating and making a positive difference in the world!

To my **Stanford classmates**, especially Karen, John, Miriam, Liam, James, and Linda—your thought-provoking questions and our shared journey as writers have helped me grow in ways I never imagined. Your talent and dedication inspire me every single day.

To my sons, **Cooper and Jack**—thank you for being extraordinary humans and the greatest teachers I could ever hope for. Words can't express the privilege of being your mom. I love you both beyond measure.

And to my beloved **Rob**—thank you for walking Fergus each morning so I could sit at my writing desk, for keeping me fueled with endless cups of piping hot coffee, and for ensuring I ate healthy meals. Most of all, thank you for being my partner in life, shenanigans and all. I love you endlessly.

This book is for all of you—you have my deepest gratitude.

ABOUT THE AUTHOR

Photo: Brenda Jankowski

Deborah Kevin is the founder and chief inspiration officer of Highlander Press, where she helps change-makers tell their stories of healing and transformation. Passionate about elevating women's voices, Debby has guided hundreds of authors to craft impactful, purpose-driven books. She's the host of the *STORYTELLHER* podcast, bringing light to women's journeys and stories. Adventurous at heart, she's trekked the Camino de Santiago and loves exploring the world with her husband, Rob, their family, and a delightful pup named Fergus. A believer in magic, a lover of French Press coffee, and a frequent user of irreverent humor, Debby brings warmth, fun, and depth to every project she touches. *Shelf Life* is her fourth nonfiction book.

instagram.com/debbykevinwriter
linkedin.com/in/deborah-kevin
youtube.com/@DeborahKevinAuthor

ABOUT THE PUBLISHER

Founded in 2019, Highlander Press is a vibrant, mid-sized publishing house dedicated to transforming the world through the power of words. We are deeply committed to diversity and bringing big ideas to the forefront. At Highlander Press, we help authors navigate the journey from initial concept through writing, editing, and publishing, culminating in the release of a book that not only fulfills a lifelong dream but also solidifies their expertise and boosts their confidence.

Join us in making a mark in the literary world, where your voice is heard, and your message has the power to change lives. Visit us at highlanderpressbooks.com to start your publishing journey.

facebook.com/highlanderpress
instagram.com/highlanderpress
linkedin.com/highlanderpress
tiktok.com/@highlanderpress